# Crumbs of Hope

# Crumbs of Hope

## Prayers from the City

Clare McBeath and
Tim Presswood

British Library Cataloguing in Publication data
A catalogue record for this book is available
from the British Library


ISBN 1-85852-310-9
ISBN 978-1-85852-310-1


First published by Inspire
4 John Wesley Road
Werrington
Peterborough PE4 6ZP


Printed and bound in Great Britain by
Aldridge Print Group, Mitcham, Surrey

# Dedication

To Saint Ida who was good news to the poor, showed her love with whisky and chocolate and will hate the fact that we call her a saint and to David Collins who looks up from the chaos of our lives and sees a laughing star.

# Acknowledgements

This book grows out of the life of our little Christian community. We are particularly grateful to the saints of Mersey Street, who are always deeply embarrassed when we call them saints!

Natalie Watson at INSPIRE originally suggested the book almost three years ago and has been a source of endless patience as well as advice and support.

Carl Whitham has taken our vague ideas for illustrations and crafted them into the beautiful images in the book for no more recompense than a plug for his studio http://www.carlwhitham.com.

The Women's Research Group to which Clare belongs has been a willing sounding board. Particular thanks go to Jan Berry for her inspiration, to Anne Phillips who allowed Clare to get away with murder and to Rachel Jenkins who still dances with us.

Finally, thanks and so much more to Deborah and Andy and our families who have put up with burned dinners, papers scattered around both our homes and who have been generally ignored in the writing of *Crumbs of Hope*.

# Contents

# Introduction: The God We Meet

As we write we are sat at the dining table in our stockinged feet amid the spilt milk and congealed Weetabix of the breakfast rush. The table has an ingrained stickiness and there are toast crumbs under the table that stick to our socks. An uncomfortable reminder that we work amid the chaos and mess that makes up our everyday lives.

The title for this book is drawn from Jesus' encounter with an unnamed Syrophoenician woman who challenges Jesus to re-think his attitude to her by demanding that even the dogs get to eat the crumbs under the table. She refuses to be ignored. She refuses to be dismissed as the dregs of society. She stands proud and claims her place. There is a dignity to her challenge. A dignity born of a hope that attitudes can change. A dignity born of a hope that social hierarchies can be different. A hope born of an encounter with a teacher who can yet be taught.

We believe there is hope. We believe there is hope that life can be different. That attitudes can change. That the Syrophoenician women of this world can stand proud and claim their place. Our hope is not triumphant or even confident. It is a hope against hope. Crumbs of hope... Crumbs of hope that in the mess of daily life we encounter God. We question, we rage, we cry but we meet with a God who shares our questions, shares our anger, shares our tears. We meet with a God who has a human face. We meet with God incarnate, birthed into the mess and din of a stable, born to a teenage, unmarried mother.

In the birth of a baby, we meet with God. In the young woman who has nowhere to live we meet with God. In the young man who questions his sexuality we meet with God. In the woman fleeing domestic violence, in the man sentenced to prison, in the children who grow up in care, in the victims of suicide bombings, in darkness and despair we meet with God. This is my body, this is my blood, do this in memory of me.

God is present in the city. God is active in the city. God is alive in the children playing in the terraced street. God is alive in the couple we married despite this being her fourth marriage. God is alive in the credit union we help to run. God is alive in the surprising glimpse of a flower growing in a crack in the wall. God is alive in falling crime rates and improving schools. God is alive in community consultations and regeneration plans.

We remember. We remember the chaos and mess of our broken world. We re-member loved ones and the unloved ones. In broken bread and spilt wine we confess our part in the brokenness around us and begin to pick up the pieces. To pick up the pieces and re-member, re-member our shattered dreams, re-member what life could be. Life. Life in its fullness. I have come that you might have life and life in all its fullness. This is my body, this is my blood.

And gathered around the table we share, share in the pain and share in the dream. Share community, share Shalom, share in the new covenant, the new relationship in God. We become community. We celebrate community.

In our case, our community consists of two families living down the road from one another, living, working, worshipping together with the tiny, vulnerable fellowship of the United Baptist Tabernacle, Higher Openshaw, Manchester. From time to time their names and stories creep into this book as a celebration of the saints of Mersey Street, as the church is more commonly known. We are a fellowship that encompasses those who have gone before, a fellowship that knows the pain and tragedy of a life cut short as Tim Clay, one of the dreamers of our community, died in a climbing accident and shattered our dreams. The day the music died. But life goes on, we pick up the pieces, we re-member, we dream.

And so we offer these prayers and eucharists, born of our lives together, born of our struggle to live in community, born of a tiny and, by the world's standards, insignificant, congregation. They have been tried and tested in our communal worship. They come out of a particular time and place.

We offer the prayers to be read, to be used, to be adapted and re-written for your own context. You may want to replace names, places and topical references with those more appropriate for your own situation. We offer them to be used individually, in small groups or congregationally, to be read by one or by several voices. If you find these prayers useful and particularly if you want to use them regularly, please get in touch via our website **www.openshawconnection.org.uk**.

We use bold print for group responses, while different 'solo' voices are indicated using roman and italic type. Specific 'instructions' are contained within square brackets and symbols are used as follows:

silence          share bread          share wine          music

All of this is merely so you know how we use the prayers. Please use them as fits your situation.

We offer these prayers in the hope that in doing so there is a deeper encounter with the God who meets us where we are in the everyday mundaneness and mess of our lives. We offer these in the hope that you too will be inspired to write, to create, to dream, to break bread and above all, to believe that there is hope. Crumbs of hope...

# Peace
## The Dream Contradicted by Reality

The view from Tim and Deborah's kitchen window looks out over their yard to the terraced houses beyond the back ginnel. One of the houses has its window frames painted a vivid orange colour and on the window ledge is lovingly placed a rather neglected and overgrown window box over-spilling with a profusion of flowers. This vibrant glimpse of hope is framed by the reality of the coil of brutal, regulation grey razor wire that 'protects' the wall.

So often our dreams are brought crashing down by the reality of the world in which we live. We want to fly, we want to dance, but our feet are made of clay, we are rooted, we are grounded in the real world. If our faith is to be meaningful then it has to be grounded in the reality of our daily life with all its struggles and contradictions.

## Sunshine and Snow

*Today it is snowing. Last week we were out in the park in our shirt sleeves. The daffodils in Tim's back yard both glint in the sunshine and weather the snow. There is something comforting even in the midst of uncertainty and change. This opening prayer celebrates the restlessness of the Spirit, both surprising us when we least expect it and challenging us to see things in a different way. But under-girding the surprise and challenge is the comforting, re-assuring Spirit of God.*

Restless Spirit of God,
You wake us up to the wonder and joy of life,
The wind rustling the new leaves of spring,
The gently falling blossom cheering a dull day,
The wind clearing out the rubbish from
    our streets,
Shaking us from our apathy and despair.

Stirring Spirit of God,
You challenge us to open our eyes,
To speak out for the hurting and vulnerable,
To hold our representatives to account,
To see the good in each person,
To nurture their possibilities and dreams.

Comforting Spirit of God,
You invite us to rest and be still,
Safe in your loving embrace,
Healed by your faith in us,
Assured that your presence is with us,
Now and always.

## Take Time to Look

*All too often we look without seeing. We drive past huge advertising hoardings without seeing how they scar our landscape. We pass barbed wire topped walls, without even noticing the fear they reveal. We see a beautiful yellow flower forcing its way through the cracks in the pavement and spray it with herbicide because someone has labelled it a weed.*

Spring time is here,
**Let us take time to look.**

The shoots push their way up through the soil,
**Let us take time to look.**

The bulbs are bursting into bloom,
**Let us take time to look.**

Nature is showing us the beauty of God,
**Let us take time to look.**

In the faces around us we glimpse the divine,
**Let us take time to look.**

# In this City

*This fast-paced prayer of approach works well if spoken rhythmically by multiple voices. The form reflects the fast-paced, disjointed nature of much inner city life, building together to form, at the end, a new 'communing'.*

In this city
we gather
together
your people
together
we gather
In this city
far away
from the fields
and the mountains
far away
from nature
we gather

| but we do not sow | We gather |
| we gather | together |
| from shops | individuals |
| from shelves | we gather |
| we gather | into a community |
| but we do not sow | together |
| we gather | into a family |
| together | we gather |
| we gather | into a relationship |
| in your presence | with one another |
| we gather | with the living God |
| broken | |

resurrection
new life
new creation
wholeness
one-ness
connection

| and cut off | We gather | We gather | We gather |
| for we have broken | this morning | this morning | in this city |
| the connection | to share our lives | to celebrate | we gather |
| between us and you | with one another | our connectedness | together |
| between ourselves | to share our lives | to share | and know that |
| and your creation | with you | and look forward | you are with us. |

# Preparing for Worship?

*This rather traditional sounding prayer of approach was written for Advent with its themes of expectation and hope. It evokes my childhood memories of grand, choir-led carol services held in a cold, traditional, candle-lit church nave. Of course this is rather far from the experience of a small church with children running around and demanding attention, ministers desperately trying to practise the music and get ready for eleven o'clock and sometimes-grumpy old people wishing that just for once they could have a 'proper' service.*

God, beyond all time and space,
We gather, humbly,
to offer you our worship,
to offer you our praise,
to offer you the best that we have
and the best that we are.
We gather, expectantly,
eager to find you,
eager to feel your love,
eager to receive your healing touch
and your forgiving acceptance.
We gather, separately,
apart from the world,
apart from the cares of everyday life,
apart from the sin which afflicts the world
and our worship.

Forgive us, Immanuel,
the times when we believe our faith can be
    separated from the rest of our lives.
Forgive us, Immanuel,
the times when we seek to worship in perfect,
    pious isolation.
Forgive us, Immanuel,
the times when we seek to keep you for
    ourselves
and to shape you in the image of our tastes
    and traditions.

Immanuel,
God with us,
Be with us
in our worship this morning
and in our leisure this afternoon.
Be with us in our labours tomorrow
and in our resting at night.
Be with us always.

# Circle of Life

*A rather eccentric chap lives directly behind our house. One summer, I saw some very suspicious plants growing in his kitchen, with constant electric light beaming onto them. A few days later, he came round to our front door to offer us three of the plants – which actually turned out to be tomatoes! What do we know of cultivation? We have a concrete back yard, not a garden. The Circle of Life is Elton John's song from Disney's Lion King. Yet it is here in the brokenness of bricks and concrete that we find God.*

In the dog days of summer,
the shadows grow long
the evenings cool
and rain creeps in to spoil
our games.

The blistering heat of July
is but a memory
a fading tan line
and a hoped-for dream.

Grapes hang heavy with juice
upon their vine
and golden wheat swells fat
upon its stalks.

The harvest is ready.

*And what do you know of harvest?*

*The bread is produced by a massive
industrial conglomerate.
Flour is traded on the international markets
and might come from anywhere the
    price is right.
The subsidies paid to western multinationals
bankrupt the farmers of the Third World.*

*Your wine cannot be produced economically
but still you think that English wine
is a delightful eccentricity
produced to keep your growers in business.*

In the dark of winter,
earth sleeps
earth shivers
earth recovers
preparing the ground
for the life to come.

And we give thanks
that our food was stored in barns and
    refrigerators
to see us through the hardship
until the firstfruits reappear.

*But you will go to the supermarket
at Christmas
to buy strawberries forced
in a far away hothouse
and flown to your table
polluting the air
killing the planet.*

*Your grapes are sprayed with sulphur
every ten days.
And fungicide every week.
Your wine is sterilized with chemicals
and filtered with fish extract.
Wine of rejoicing. Wine of forgetting.*

Then when hope has almost died
spring brings new life.
Spring brings daffodils, lambs
and the chirruping of newly hatched birds.

The trees put on their summer clothing
green and youthful
smiling as the rains wash away
the memory of dark winter.

*And in your city streets*
*how much spring do you see?*
*Does the grass break through the tarmac?*
*Do the factories stop belching out their*
    *death-giving fumes*
*and breathe instead the rain-soaked*
    *morning air?*

*Do the supermarkets heave a sigh of relief*
*as the store-cupboard provisions*
*are replenished with the first new season's*
    *vegetables?*

*Do you taste with joy*
*the first of last year's new wine*
*hoping it will be good*
*or do you buy another bottle*
*of industrially perfected New World*
    *Chardonnay?*

In the dog days of summer,
the shadows grow long
the evenings cool
and rain creeps in to spoil
our games.

The blistering heat of July
is but a memory
a fading tan line
and a hoped-for dream.

Grapes hang heavy with juice
upon their vine
and golden wheat swells fat
upon its stalks.

The harvest is ready
and the table of celebration is spread.

*But what are we celebrating?*
*Bread is sold and bought,*
*some have bread, many do not.*
*For some the harvest does not come.*

On the night before the tree of life
became the tree of death
Jesus took bread
lovingly he gave thanks
before he ripped it apart
and gave it to them.

*Here I am. Broken,*
*to share in your brokenness,*
*to share in your hunger,*
*Do this in memory of me*
*to share in my brokenness.*

On the night before the sunlit sky
turned dark as night
Jesus took a jug of wine
lovingly he gave thanks
before he poured it out
and gave it to them.

*Never forget.*
*Never take for granted the Life*
*you have been given.*
*Do this in celebration of my life*
*to celebrate the circle of life.*

**AND THERE WILL BE GLORIOUS SUMMER**

# Enough Room for Everyone

*We worship in the middle of a late Victorian estate of 'two-up, two-down' terraces fronting directly onto the street. Film makers have often used our community as a backdrop to portray a stereotyped view of 'gritty northern reality'. Children play in the road because they have nowhere else to go. In summer people sunbathe on front doorsteps. Space is at a premium.*

*So it is with Mersey Street itself. Church is full of what you or I might consider to be rubbish, but which has been lovingly preserved. This is not re-cycling in its modern sense, but rather the old fashioned 'make do and mend' environmentalism which preserved everything because 'you never know when it'll come in handy'.*

We praise you our Loving God,
for creating an earth with enough room for everyone,
where nature sustains environments of harmony and balance,
where new life springs out of death and decay,
where adaptation and change bring new possibilities.

We praise you our Loving God,
for the gift of your son identified with our humanity,
who welcomes the outcast and the lost,
who does not see the world as we see it,
but proclaims peace and justice for all.

We praise you our Loving God,
for the exuberance and wisdom of your spirit,
who invites us to move on in our journey of faith,
who challenges us to forgiveness and reconciliation,
and sends us out to live our lives as part of the solution.

# The Cost of Following: The Cost of Not-following

*We are not good at confession. Perhaps this is the evangelical fear of catholic ritual. Perhaps it is a reluctance to further de-value people whose self-esteem is already low. Here an individual confession leads us into an understanding of the corporate nature of sin and its devastating results for our world.*

Jesus says, Come
Follow me.
We say,
In a minute,
I just need to finish my work.

Jesus says, Come
Follow me.
We say,
Can't you ask someone else?
I've got so much to do.

Jesus says, Come
Follow me.
We say,
But you're not going
The way that I want to go.

When we walk our own paths
Forgive us
When we choose death over life
Forgive us
When war seems easier than negotiation
Forgive us
When profit comes before justice
Forgive us
When greed makes us squander resources
Forgive us
When we walk our own paths
Forgive us

Jesus says, Come
Follow me.

Amen

# What Is on the Inside

Loving God,
When we get angry
**Gather us in.**

When we go off in a sulk
**Gather us in.**

When we fail to see the bigger picture
**Gather us in.**

Help us to put aside our differences and divisions
**Gather us together to worship you.**

Loving God,
When we have a temper tantrum or go off and sulk
**Thank you that you still love us and want the best for us.**

When we are selfish and don't think of others
**Thank you that you still love us and want the best for us.**

When we are down on ourselves
**Thank you that you still love us and want the best for us.**

When we exclude someone else because of their looks or behaviour
**Help us to see it is what is on the inside that counts.**

When we don't make the effort to be someone's friend
**Help us to see it is what is on the inside that counts.**

When people are shy and lacking in confidence,
**Help us to see it is what is on the inside that counts.**

# The Gallery

*On the wall behind the communion table hangs a brightly painted Salvadoran cross. We brought it back from El Salvador to remind us of the tiny El Cordero de Dios congregation who were, in so many ways, similar to us, but who had lived through hardships and persecutions that we could not imagine. It was in the lives of these very ordinary people that we found the God of hope.*

*Palm Sunday contrasts the expectations of "Messiah" with the reality of a carpenter on a donkey, so this year we decided to make our own 'Salvadoran' cross by cutting up photographs of our everyday life together and pasting them onto a rather gluey wallpaper cross.*

*This eucharist holds all these ideas together by contrasting the pomp and formality of many art galleries with the life which is found within the pictures themselves.*

The gallery
is dark
enclosed
womb-like
oppressively
silent
pictures hung
with reverence
severe
imposing
gilded frames
proclaiming
their status
lights dimmed
for fear
of deterioration.

The oil
lies thick
on canvas
plastered
from an
artist's
palette
carved out
with a knife
hues hang heavy
stagnant
lifeless
people
posed
in a stilted
costume drama.

The gallery
is dark
enclosed
womb-like
rhythmic music
sounds
a gentle heartbeat
pictures
leap out
hung with
joyful
reverence
spotlights
jar provocatively
bringing
pictures to life.

The colours leap
with vibrancy
inviting discussion
laughter
disagreement
as the rabble
processes chaotically
footprints joining
rhythmic heartbeat
in a pilgrimage
of discovery
a canvas of life
refusing to be
constrained
by the limits
of a frame.

The procession
continues
crowds cheering
donkey hooves
clip clopping
the rush
of palms
waving
in the breeze
bright cloaks
in textured
fabrics
reminder
of ordinary folk's
collage of
layered lives.

The picture
draws
inwards
almost
hidden
in the midst
of the crowds
a figure
legs dangling
below a
donkey's belly
a simple
roughly dressed
man
the centre of
fuss and acclaim.

Not the great
marbled
halls
where pictures
hang
dead and lifeless
in semi darkness
protected
by cameras
and wires
that screech
alarms
on the gentlest
of brushes
off limits
out of bounds.

The picture
is familiar
everyday life
our selves
staring back
from the layers
of canvas
but behind
the riotous colour
and soundscapes
is a hint
an undercurrent
the menace
of violence
lurking in
the wings.

Ripping
tearing
searing hatred
the picture hangs
in shreds
jagged edged
fibres, yarns
spilling
blood red
across
our lives
body broken
blood shed
life spent
grief
uniting humanity.

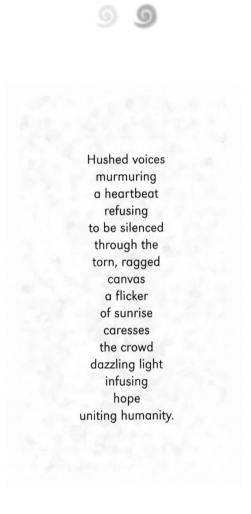

Hushed voices
murmuring
a heartbeat
refusing
to be silenced
through the
torn, ragged
canvas
a flicker
of sunrise
caresses
the crowd
dazzling light
infusing
hope
uniting humanity.

# Waters of Despair

*Living in the shadow of 'regeneration', never being quite sure whether your home will be demolished or not, together with the grinding stress of poverty, fear of crime and the other joys of living in the inner city, mental health has become something of a theme. We have run a number of mental health related projects. Perhaps the most notable of these are the complementary therapies offered in the 'sanctuary' of the church. Relaxing to some gentle music while having an aromatherapy massage, surrounded by the artwork and other debris left over from Sunday worship has held back the waters of despair for many of us.*

When the dark of winter makes scarce the sun
**Come to the living God**

When the burdens we carry weigh us down
**Come to the living God**

When the waters of despair threaten to cover the earth
**Come to the living God**

Come to the living God
**who was there from before the foundations of the earth**
**who says I will give you rest**
**and brings light to the darkest place.**

# Waiting in the Womb

*I have given birth not once, but twice in the last five years, both life changing and profound experiences that have not just shaped my life but turned it upside down. The messy reality of birth is not something we usually remember or celebrate in our worship. We give thanks for the new life of a baby and pray for parents embarking on this new stage of learning to be a family, but rarely do we even acknowledge the fear, pain or miracle of birth itself, which seems strange as being born is the one experience that unites us all. One time in the Christian year where pregnancy and birth can be spoken of is during the season of Advent when we all await the messiness and reality of a new birth, Immanuel, God with us.*
*This prayer was co-written with David Sutcliffe.*

Too tired to sleep,
seeing darkness,
the room embracing,
remembering dreams,
life's story held in trust.

Open-eyed in darkness,
invisible, yet a heart beats,
individual, yet dependent,
expectation of a mystery,
a new beginning stretches into eternity.

Waiting God,
waiting in the darkness and security of the womb,
waiting for the first pains of labour,
waiting for the moment, the messiness of birth,
waiting impatiently, birthing the miracle of new life.

Waiting God,
wait with us in our fears and insecurities,
wait with us through our pain and confusion,
wait with us in the chaos of our distorted, violent world,
birth in us the miracle of recreated lives.

# Rachel's Hymn

*It seems a very long time ago that Tim and Deborah's beautiful baby Rachel was born and 'presented' at church. It was – she is now thirteen. In those days we still had not only an organ but an organist to play it! Hence the somewhat traditional feel to this hymn. It could go to any Common Metre tune.*

1. We come to praise the living God,
   made flesh before our eyes;
   in human likeness here displayed,
   the one God of Surprise.

2. The love of God was born a child,
   and in a manger laid;
   the image of the living God
   in every child displayed.

3. Where two disciples meet, or three,
   so Christ is with them there;
   we claim that promise in his name
   and our rejoicing share.

4. As to the temple, Jesus went,
   we bring our child today
   to thank God for her precious life
   and bless her on her way.

5. So may our home become a place,
   where dwells the heavenly dove,
   where we may celebrate life's gift
   and always work for love.

# Joy of New Life

*This prayer was written for my daughter Imogen's Naming and Blessing Ceremony which we held among friends and family in our overgrown city garden on a beautiful summer's day. As she was just a few months old, I had no idea then of how her personality would develop so this prayer was very much about celebrating potential and possibility.*

Creating Spirit,
We give you thanks...
for the wonder and joy of new life,
for the grasping of tiny fingers,
for feet kicking with excitement,
for the blowing of bubbles.

Nurturing Spirit,
We give you thanks...
for the growing of soft, downy hair,
for cries of discomfort and delight,
for the sound of gentle breathing,
for smiles and plenty of giggles.

Impatient Spirit,
We give you thanks...
for the scrunching and chewing of paper,
for the pulling of hair and the poking of ears,
for the fun of rolling over and over,
for the humour of copying facial expressions.

Creating, Nurturing, Impatient Spirit,
We give you thanks...
for the birth of this new life,
for (name) who is changing our lives,
daughter, sister, grandchild, great grandchild,
Godchild, niece, cousin, new friend.

Through this miracle of new life may we draw closer to you, O Giver of Life.

# Lord of the Dance

*The term 'Lord' has a somewhat chequered history. In a church made up mostly of women, and where deprivation and poverty are all too common, 'Lord' does not seem a helpful image to use of God. At Clare's ordination, we deliberately re-wrote the vows she would make to avoid using this term. Sydney Carter's marvellous hymn uses Lord in a more liberating way. The Lord of the dance is akin to the medieval Lord of Misrule, playful and mischievous, setting the spirit free, rather than enslaving her.*

Lord of the dance

We bring before you those who cannot dance
because they have no joy

We bring before you those who will not dance
because they are too busy with their own importance

We bring before you those for whom dancing
is an undreamed of luxury

And those whose lives are filled with
empty dancing, who dance to forget

We pray for those whose pains or age
stop them from dancing

And for those who are told they
cannot dance

# Fire and Ice

*February is always a bit of a low time. Christmas is a distant memory and Easter still seems a long way off. So this particular February Tim and I decided we needed a festival and Candlemas, or Imbolc, seemed to fit the bill. Its themes of the warmth of God's love and the looking for the signs of the coming of the spring provided inspiration and a source of festivity. As a symbol for Candlemas, we used a fantastic glass bowl filled with ice, in the centre of which a candle was placed giving a beautiful orangey pink glow glinting through the ice.*

Divine Wanderer,
We praise you for welcoming us to your world,
for the love and companionship of our families and friends,
for the people we meet when we're down at the shops,
for the acceptance and hospitality of our little church community.

Divine Fire,
We praise you for the crackle of fires in the hearth,
for the warmth and beauty of the winter sun,
for the glimpses of new life we see in the streets around us,
for the signs of hope we catch in the faces of people we meet.

Divine Life,
We praise you for the beauty of winter,
for the cold glint of icicles hanging from drain pipes,
for the icing-sugar-snow dusting the back yards of our houses,
for the new green shoots bursting up from the ground.

Divine Inspiration,
We praise you for the moments of fun and laughter,
for the children making puppets and telling stories,
for the energy and imagination of local communities,
for the dreams and visions we nurture and offer tentatively to others.

# Journeying Towards the Cross

*I was asked to help lead worship for the International Academy of Practical Theology conference and can still picture distinguished international theologians processing around the worship space singing and waving coloured ribbons and streamers as we turned our thoughts to the theme of journeying towards the cross.*

We have met and journeyed together,
let us go now on our separate paths,
journeying onwards towards the cross.
Let us weep where Jesus weeps,
speak out where Jesus speaks out,
keep vigil where Jesus keeps vigil,
and let us hope
for the rising of the Easter dawn.

# Harvest for the World

*Yesterday we had a conversation with our church secretary, David. He was very distressed because walking past a local youth club, he had been accosted by a gang of youths, all wearing BNP badges and some even swastikas. This area has seen an influx of refugees in the last few years. For the most part, they have been welcomed as bringing some much needed stability. Nevertheless, there is simmering racism under the surface, and the BNP are targeting our community.*
*This eucharist was originally written for Racial Justice Sunday, which was also our harvest festival – we never have quite got the idea of a calendar right!*

When will there be...?
When will there be peace for the world?
When will there be justice for the world?
When will there be a harvest for the world?
When will there be...?

This is the longing that we bring to this table
This is the hope that we bring to this meal
This is the vision that this communion points us towards
This is the taste of heaven that we celebrate here

This is the table where all are invited
This is the meal where no one comes first
This is the communion that reaches across barriers
This is the taste of heaven where different races and cultures join together

Yet we know that the table of sharing is not always reality
Yet we know that often this meal is governed by rules which exclude
Yet we know in our hearts that we fail to live up to the spirit of communion
Yet we know that many never get to experience the taste of heaven

 [play Harvest for the World by the Isley Brothers or the Christians]

So we come to this table
Those of us whose faith is too certain and too secure
Those of us whose faith is vulnerable and hangs in the balance
We come bringing our fears and insecurities
We come bringing our failings and prejudices
We represent the people of our broken world

We represent the hope of our world's longing for justice
We come to celebrate the vision of God's Shalom
We come to share in a taste of heaven on earth

And as we share we give thanks for the bread
made of many grains just as many races make up our world
And as the dough has to be worked together
so we too commit to working together for racial justice
And we give thanks for the wine
made by the crushing of grapes to represent the violence of our world
And as the wine is poured out in love
so we too ask that we would be filled with your love for all people

On the night Jesus was betrayed
a diverse group gathered around a table
On the night before Jesus was put to death
he shared a last meal
breaking bread and saying,
'This is my body broken for you.
Do this in memory of me'

On the night before the temple curtain was ripped apart
wine was poured
On the night before a soldier looked into the face of God
wine was shared
Jesus saying,
'This wine is the new relationship sealed by my blood.
Do this in memory of me'

As we eat this bread let us remember the racism and abuse that many people experience

As we drink this wine let us celebrate the diversity and richness brought by people of different races cultures and religions

When will there be...?
When will there be peace for the world?
When will there be justice for the world?
When will there be a harvest for the world?
When will there be...?

This is the longing that we bring to this table
This is the hope that we bring to this meal
This is the vision that this communion points us towards
This is the taste of heaven that we celebrate here

# Longing for Peace

*We long for peace. We believe one day there will be peace. We foolishly and stubbornly hope there might be peace – what more can we say?*

God who longs for peace,
We live in a divided and broken world,
a world where people march not for peace...
but to proclaim their sectarianism;
a world where people have lost faith in
    political protest...
and resort to blowing up themselves
    and the neighbours they hate;
a world where soldiers are called
    peace-keepers...
and bombs are dropped in the name of
    national and international security.

**God who longs for peace...**
**Give us the wisdom to see both sides**
    **of the story.**

God who longs for justice,
We live in an unfair and unjust world,
a world where supermarkets get bigger and
    bigger...
while local farmers grow poorer and poorer;
a world where the haves get richer and richer...
and the have nots have less and less;
a world where the centre of the industrial
    revolution...
lies polluted and half derelict, yet still we do
    not learn.

**God who longs for justice...**
**Give us the courage to challenge**
    **our unjust systems.**

God who longs for healing and wholeness,
We live in a world which is fragile and broken,
a world where species are dying and
    becoming extinct...
while we continue to pollute and destroy
    their habitats;
a world where victims are forced to relive
    their terror...
if they are ever to receive justice from our
    courts;
a world of vicious circles where the abused...
all too easily become the abusers of
    themselves or others.

**God who longs for healing and wholeness...**
**Give us the love to persevere**
    **when all else fails.**

In the name of the one who dares us to dream
    peace into being,
in the name of the one who shows us creative
    ways to challenge injustice,
and in the name of the one whose love
    embraces all.

# Offering
## Telling the Story that Gives Life

Mersey Street has quite a tradition of story telling. It is not uncommon, during a service, for a member of the congregation, young or old, to launch off into a story vaguely connected to the theme of the service or to start to re-tell a biblical story from a different perspective. It is our way of valuing our past and expressing our identity in the present in order to dream our future into being. Here, this story telling tradition is celebrated in our own version of a Salvadoran Cross.

As a small church we are often privileged to receive gifts from others. We are grateful to receive. But we also need to be allowed to give without expecting in return. Maybe our gifts are not so much monetary gifts but the gift we make of ourselves. We offer our stories, our past, our present and our future to be shaped as part of God's story of incarnation and redemption.

# You Really Are with Us

*This prayer, which could be used either at the beginning or end of worship or both, was written as a reminder that God is present with us throughout the chaos of our day, with us in the tears, tantrums, the rustle of sweet papers, whoops of delight and incessant questions; God with us.*

In the darkness of
   the night
**You are with us**
In the tiredness of early
   morning
**You are with us**
In the pain of aching bones
**You are with us**
In the sweet sip of
   morning tea
**You are with us**
In the rush of breakfast
**You are with us.**

Now
Here
In this place
You are with us.

And as we go out
**You are with us**
In preparing lunch
**You are with us**
In the business of the afternoon
**You are with us**
In sticking and the gluing
**You are with us**

In the visiting of friends
**You are with us**
In the grumpy teatime quarrels
**You are with us**
In bedtime stories and cuddles
**You are with us**
In the blessed relief of sleep
**You are with us**
In the darkness of the night
**You are with us.**

**EVER-PRESENT GOD
BE WITH US NOW**

# Everlasting One

*Last year Tim and I had a surprising phone call to ask whether we would be willing to feature as part of that year's Baptist 'Home Mission' video celebrating the church's survival in the inner city. The presenter chose to interview Ida and David during which he made the mistake of asking what had sustained them all these years, to which the reply came back 'We'd no flaming option!'*

Come, let us gather before the faithful God,
the everlasting One who has travelled with her people
across the bounds of time and place,
through birth, growth and death,
weaving in and out of the joy and pain of our lives.

Come, let us gather before the faithful God,
the everlasting One who calls us to share our journey,
through the decades, wherever we find ourselves,
from our beginning to our departing,
as we weave the joy and pain of our lives together.

## Keep Us Keeping on

*The video was previewed at the Baptist Assembly where it was wonderful to see Ida and David talking about their faithful refusal to close the church and their hopes and fears about the future. This was picked up in the keynote address which focused on the theme of Keep On Keeping On. For one brief moment it felt as though we were able to offer something important to the wider church.*

 [chant – such as 'I waited, I waited on the Lord' – Wild Goose Worship Group, *Heaven Shall Not Wait*]

Faithful God
We thank you that you don't give up on us
**Keep us keeping on**

Give us the patience not to give up on you
**Keep us keeping on**

When the time ahead is uncertain
**Keep us keeping on**

When progress seems slow or non-existent
**Keep us keeping on**

When we are weary of working within the system
**Keep us keeping on**

When the challenges of our world seem too great
**Keep us keeping on**

When the burden of caring gets us down
**Keep us keeping on**

When we are tired and worn out
**Hold us in your love.**

## Shrek

*Clare didn't want to include this opening prayer in this book at all. It is very simple and silly. It also speaks of a reality which affects all too many people today, when images of perfect beauty oppress young girls into believing that only a supermodel figure makes them beautiful. Shrek, the ogre, turns out to be the most beautiful of all.*

Mirror, Mirror on the wall,
Who's the fairest of them all?
Mirror, Mirror on the wall
I don't think I'm worth anything
    at all!

**God who creates us in your**
    **own image,**
**You hold us and hug us**
**and love us for who we are.**
**Gather us together this morning**
**that we may reflect your beauty**
**to ourselves,**
**to each other**
**and beyond.**

Mirror, Mirror on the wall,
God loves each one of us all.

30

# Upside Down God

*I like Palm Sunday. It speaks to me of a world whose values are upside down, where riches and political power are valued above love and self-giving. It tells a story of a God who confronts the everyday reality of a world corrupted by global capitalism, and of a faith which does not seek an escape from the world around it, but rather which attempts to change it.*

Upside down God,
Hear us now, as we pray for your world,
as we pray for our world.

In a world of binge drinking and Saturday
    night escapism,
teach us to celebrate achievements.
In a world of celebrity and fame,
teach us to value the quiet.
In a world of politics and power,
teach us to ask your questions.

Upside down God,
**Turn our swords into ploughshares,
    and give us your peace.**

In a world of money and consumption,
share with us your poverty.
In a world of waste and plenty,
share with us your self-giving love.
In a world where the poor scavenge a living
    from our rubbish,
share with us your thankful generosity.

Upside down God,
**Turn our swords into ploughshares,
    and give us your peace.**

In a world where children grow up
    on the street,
let us come unto you.
In a world where women are degraded
    and devalued,
let us wash your feet with our tears.
In a world where the unemployed
    serve no purpose,
let us set out on your mission.

Upside down God,
**Turn our swords into ploughshares,
    and give us your peace.**

**Palm Sunday God,
fold the palm leaves of our triumphalism
into the cross of discipleship
and teach us to follow you
to the fullness of your Shalom.**

# God Who Treasures the Small

*She had endured a very violent marriage, but still yearned for the husband who had died over ten years earlier. Whenever she came into church, she spoke effusively about her family, but in reality lived almost entirely alone and unvisited. She loved to talk. She loved to talk and rarely had the opportunity to do so, so when she came into church, it was hard to shut her up – even during prayers! How important it was, then, for our local primary school to invite her to come in and befriend the nine- and ten-year-olds of Year 5, to have a cup of tea and a biscuit and to have an opportunity to tell stories – and be their living history project.*

God who treasures the small,

The world dictates everything must be bigger, better, faster...
yet walking and cycling are healthier for us and for the environment,
consuming less means there is more to share with others,
and shopping locally helps strengthen our community.

**Teach us to see the greatness of the small.**

The world says power belongs to the young, the ambitious, the wealthy...
yet the children of a primary school invite us to share our experience,
local residents have a voice in regeneration board meetings,
and vegetables are growing outside the Houses of Westminster.

**Teach us to see the greatness of the small.**

The world listens to those with influence, media access, and technology...
yet Tanzanian officials speak of the importance of Jubilee 2000 chains,
a college recognizes the voices of prophecy speaking from the inner city,
and a church building receives a face-lift from those on community service.

**Teach us to see the greatness of the small.**

# Grounded God

*Leaving church one evening, a vulnerable old lady in her eighties was attacked by a gang of local teenagers. Although physically unhurt, she was so terrified that she felt unable to come back. Around the same time, the church garden was vandalized, plants lovingly tended were ripped up and scattered around. David began to repair the damage. Seeing this, it was one of the local teenage lads – probably playing hookey from the high school behind church – who stopped and offered to help David to replant the daffodils. The unlikely couple – a beautiful old man, and a lovely young truant – spent a happy hour or so together planting bulbs.*

Grounded God,
You have gathered us together;
gathered us from our scattered homes,
our scattered communities,
from our different backgrounds,
our different lifestyles.
Gathered us at this time, in this space,
around this your table,
a glimpse of heaven,
touching the messy reality of earth.

Here heaven and earth meet...
in the giggling laughter of a child at play,
in two men sharing lunch on a
    city-centre bench,
in a teenager replanting bulbs that
    vandals have uprooted,
in a new mum and an eighty-year-old
    sharing life's experiences.

Here we catch a glimpse of God...
as neighbours work to create a
    community garden,
as a class of children listen to the memories
    of older residents,
as a congregation risk abuse and insults
    to keep a building open,
as we share in the pain and hopes that follow
    a Salvadoran earthquake.

Rooted God,
You gather us as scattered people,
from the brokenness of our everyday lives.
Forgive us when we get despondent
    and lose heart,
when we cling to what is secure and fail to
    take a risk.
Forgive us when close our eyes to the pain
    and needs of the world,
and for when we fail to see you at work
    in those around us.
Open our eyes to see where heaven
    touches earth.
Open our hearts to catch a glimpse of you
    made flesh among us.

33

# Can Anything Good Come out of...?

*On this particular Sunday the lectionary texts focused on the question from the opening chapter of John's gospel, 'Can anything good come out of Nazareth?' This was teamed with the story of Samuel and Eli and led us to focus on the experience of our own community where the old and the young are not particularly valued. As this is what Mersey Street itself looks like, we focused on valuing ourselves as a community and looking at stories of people such as Rosa Parks, who in valuing themselves and in going about their daily lives made a radical difference not just to their own communities but to the shape of the story of humanity.*

Can anything good come out of...
the musings of Eli,
an elderly man whose sight was failing,
yet who discerned the voice of God calling?

Can anything good come out of...
the elderly members of our own community,
who share their experiences and wisdom,
who show us how to live in community by their welcome and hospitality?

We thank you and pray for the older people we know,
as they struggle with the challenges of age and failing health.
Help them to continue to discern your voice in their lives.

Can anything good come out of...
the naivety of Samuel,
a young boy who showed enormous courage
in speaking the prophetic word in his community?

Can anything good come out of...
the children in our own community,
whose lives often lack nurturing and stability,
yet who challenge us with their desire to make the world a better place?

We thank you and pray for the children we know
as they learn how to survive in the harsh realities of our world.
Help them to treasure their sense of wonder and dreams of justice and peace.

Can anything good come out of...
a refugee family from Nazareth,
the son of a tradesman
who turns our world's values upside down with his stories and teachings?

Can anything good come out of...
the ordinary folk in our own community,
the low paid workers, the single mums, the unemployed, the asylum seekers,
who challenge us by their involvement to re-write the stories of government and power?

We thank you and pray for the residents and leaders in our own community,
as together we seek to regenerate and recreate our community.
Help us to keep hope alive as we work towards making our visions a reality.

Can anything good come out of...
a woman refusing to give up her seat,
as Rosa Parks became the catalyst for the bus boycotts
and the end of segregation and oppression in the Southern States?

Can anything good come out of...
the campaigns against racism and oppression,
the movements for fair trade and peace,
that we are involved with in our own small way?

We thank you and pray for the work of organizations and individuals
who campaign on justice and peace issues,
holding our governments, banks, companies and ourselves to account.

Can anything good come out of...
one man's assassination 2000 years ago
out of brokenness and grief, humility and despair?
It is from these that new life, that resurrection springs.

Can anything good come out of...
gathering together around this table, breaking bread and sharing wine?
It is here that we celebrate the hope of a new relationship with God and with one another.
It is here we taste the possibilities of heaven touching earth.

# Give and Take

*A group once met at Mersey Street for what was to prove a very difficult and painful 'political' meeting with the very angry members of our congregation. Our anger, however, was carefully channelled. Instead of a fight, we offered lunch. Instead of argument, we told stories. Having resolved the issues, one of their number spotted one of the many sideboards which adorn the church. This, he decided, would be perfect to keep his tools in. The sideboard was somehow manoeuvred out and into his car.*

**Blessed be you, God,**
who makes the sun to shine.
**Blessed be you, God,**
who makes the rain to fall.

**Blessed be you, God,**
who makes the cities roar.
**Blessed be you, God,**
who makes the country still.

**Blessed be you, God,**
who makes the crops to grow.
**Blessed be you, God,**
who shapes the world with human skill.

**Blessed be you, God,**
who gives bread to eat.
**Blessed be you, God,**
who gives wine to drink.

**Blessed be you, God,**
who feeds Israel's chosen son.
**Blessed be you, God,**
who feeds Palestine's outcast daughter.

**Blessed be you, God,**
who shines upon Chechnya's darkness.
**Blessed be you, God,**
who lightens the Russian night.

**Blessed be you, God,**
who showers privilege upon the USA.
**Blessed be you, God,**
who pours love on Afghanistan's poverty.

Yours, God, is the greatness.
Yours, God, is the justice.
Yours, God, is the mercy.

And ours, we confess, is the brokenness.

On the night we betrayed him, Jesus took a
piece of bread and when he had given thanks,
he tore it apart for the life of the world. This is
my body; my very life, torn apart for your sin.

After supper he took the wine of rejoicing and
poured it out for humankind. Drink, not to
forget, but to remember. Remember that in my
brokenness there will be wholeness.

This is my promise.
For ever.

For ever
and ever.

Now
and for all time.

Hope.

Hope in me.

Hope in each other.
Hope and believe.

Believe that the lion will lie down with the lamb.
That swords will be ploughshares.
That trade will be fair.
That our community will be reborn.

Believe in life before death.

**We have shared the poor's bread.**
**We have taken wine from the oppressed.**
**We have been filled with their hope**
**And your love.**
**Make us worthy of what we have received.**

# Temptation

*Sometimes it is tempting to take the 'easy' road, to give in and pretend to be a 'proper' church. A colleague from another church reflected on his church's homelessness projects and ministry of welcome for the stranger. Nevertheless, he used the language of 'failure' because of its continued decline in worshipping numbers. Faithfully following Jesus out into the wilderness has not led to a 'successful' church. Language and images of 'Satan' are not ones we use often but provide a powerful metaphor for the temptation to take up the offer of power and glory, to look for bread made from stones. Instead Jesus calls us out of our certainties and security into the wilderness and bewilderedness of our world. Blessed is the one who does not turn stones into bread!*

Satan stands before us now
and offers us power and glory
Satan stands before us now
and offers us faith which can never fail
Satan stands before us now
and offers us bread made from stones

Jesus calls us to follow

Satan offers a church
a fellowship
a gathering
of like-minded friends
singing their songs
praying their prayers
safe
secure
in the presence of their god

Jesus calls us to follow

Jesus calls us to follow him
out into the wilderness
to leave our nets
to leave our homes
to leave our comfort and security
and follow him

out into the wilderness,
out into the bewilderedness
of faith.

Faith in the God
who offers no answers,
but shares in our questions
who does not prevent our suffering
but knows the pain of our hunger
who doesn't lift us above this world,
but hangs on a cross.

So come, gather
you who are weak
come, gather
you who are lost
come, gather
you who do not quite know
why you are here.

Jesus does not call you here
to escape from the world
but to share with him
in bread
and wine
in body
and blood.

38

the stones do not turn to bread

the stones thrown at gun-wielding soldiers
the stones thrown through old women's
    windows
the stones thrown in judgement
of those whom we catch

the stones do not turn to bread

For our bread is the body of Christ
the body given in love
the body broken
For our body is the body of Christ.

For, on a night like so many others
a night of violence and betrayal
Jesus gathered with those who would
    follow him
This is my body, broken for you.
When you break bread,
remember the story of my brokenness.

And at that moment of despair
when all hope was lost
when all friendship was betrayed
This is my blood, shed with profligate waste
This is my blood, flowing in promise
Lo, I am with you to the end of the age.

And in that promise
And in that covenant
our fasting turns to feasting
our sorrow to joy
and even our stones cry out loud:

**Holy, holy, holy**
**God of vulnerability and love**
**Heaven and earth are filled with**
    **your gentleness**
**Hosanna in the lowliest places**

Blessed is the One, who does not turn stones
    into bread
Hosanna in the lowliest places.

**Transforming God**
**send your spirit upon us**
**and upon this bread and wine.**
**Transform, not stones into bread**
**but us into disciples**
**proclaiming your Peace**
**in a world of violence**
**proclaiming your Hope**
**in a world of despair.**

# The Call of Wisdom

*This prayer was written as a contemporary expression of the opening verse of Proverbs 8, where Wisdom is depicted roaming the town issuing her call to all who will listen.*

Wisdom has built her house,
she has hewn her seven pillars,
and set her table before us.

Wisdom calls,
calls from the highest places,
from the newly repainted, 1960s tower blocks
from the multi-storey car parks and
    shopping arcades.

Wisdom searches,
searches to the ends of the earth,
from the boarded up terraced houses,
to the park railings and street corners.

Wisdom seeks,
seeks out those who desire understanding,
who value wisdom more than the latest
    mobile phone,
knowledge more than digital TV.

So come, listen for the whisper of Wisdom,
for the voice of insight and understanding.
Come gather at her table and share
    of her fruits,
of bread and wine, the offerings of earth.

We come responding to Wisdom's call,
to dwell in her house and feast at her table.

# Hymns

*For the times when we are away the congregation have developed what they call 'Hymn Services'. Somehow, with no musician, they struggle through some of their favourite old hymns and David weaves stories and reflections in and among the hymns. Usually, these are stories that have become the mythology of who we are as a community, the church's story, re-told for now.*
*This storytelling tradition values our past and serves as the foundation for moving on into the future. It is also an offering which we, small and vulnerable as we may be, are able to make to the wider Christian community.*

Loving God,
We are here in the quiet and the stillness,
we are here in the sounds of children playing,
we are here in the noises of the city streets
    around us,
to worship you.

We are here where people have worshipped
    over generations,
we are here gathered out of the business of
    our own lives,
we are here to dream the future into being,
we are here to worship you.

In the great hymns of the past that
    awaken memories,
in the music that reminds us of the events
    in our lives,
in the new songs that we learn together,
we worship you.

# Here in the Modern City

*Sometimes worship materials are born out of sheer desperation. A couple of years after we arrived in this community, I faced once again, with some dread, 'harvest' festival. Tables at the front of church were filled with fresh fruit and vegetables. Offerings were made with some generosity and the service clearly meant something to the congregation. But not to me. We don't plough the fields and scatter.*

1. Here in the modern city,
    we have no fields to plough;
   Our food is grown by others
    and comes, we know not how;
   And yet we want to offer
    our harvest praise today,
   For still in God's creation
    we have our part to play.

    *All good gifts around us*
     *are sent from heaven above,*
    *Then thank the Lord,*
     *O thank the Lord,*
    *For all his love.*

2. We place our trust in money,
    and in the welfare state;
   But these we know are human
    so justice has to wait;
   The harvest is unequal
    and some, they have no bread.
   O help us to keep working
    'til all your folk are fed.

3. So at this time of harvest
    our grateful thanks we sing;
   The firstfruits of our labours,
    our lives an offering.
   Let's plant the seed of justice
    and work that it might grow,
   Until God's love eternal,
    on earth its fruit shall show.

# Miriam's Sister

*This prayer was written for my friend Jill's ordination which focused around a fantastic 'story-telling' drawn from the Miriam narrative. Jill asked me to co-write with her friend Jess Uden, who as well as being ten at the time also lived at the other end of the country. Jess and I devised a way of co-writing via e-mail, first identifying themes and then Jess responding practically and in prose to my musings around the character of Miriam. You might want to replace Jess' responses with responses from your own context.*

Singing, dancing, making music with her people,
Miriam celebrates on the farthest shores of the Red Sea,
Her people at last free from slavery and injustice.

Crying, mourning, lamenting with their people,
Egypt's sisters grieve on the near shores of the Red Sea,
When will we learn that conflict bears no winners?

*We especially pray for the children in Northern Ireland who have had to come through violent streets on the way to school over the last week. We should also think about Israelis and Palestinians as they struggle to come to agreements about land.*

**God of our past, present and future generations, help us to see both sides of the story.**

Strong, brave, daring to speak out,
Miriam is not afraid to think for herself,
Paying the price for saying that something isn't right.

Prophet and leader, outcast from her community,
But prepared to be reconciled,
Miriam finds a welcome among her people.

*We pray for the refugees and asylum seekers that have been on the news lately as they struggle to find countries and homes that respect and want them. We pray for people who welcome and home refugees and for people who have a hard heart towards them.*

**God of our past, present and future generations, help us to be welcoming towards others.**

Gifted, enthusiastic, a creative leader,
Miriam guides and encourages her people,
In their journeying with you.

Speaking out against injustice,
Daring to be unpopular,
Miriam acts out of love and compassion.

*We pray for (name) as she begins her ministry! Thank you for her smile. Remind her she is never alone in what she does in her work for you. We pray for the churches in this community and the wider church.*

**God of our past, present and future generations, help us to challenge injustice.**

Longing, waiting, suffering with her people,
Miriam sees through Pharaoh's schemes,
Creatively subverting power and authority.

Watching over a baby on the River Nile,
Gently suggesting a caring solution,
Miriam ministers to her people.

*Let's stop for a few minutes and think about the homeless begging and selling the* Big Issue *on the street. We should also think about those who are ill and those who are looking after them. Make people stronger as they miss loved ones they have lost. And lastly we pray for ourselves and our families.*

**God of our past, present and future generations, hold us in the palm of your hand.**

# The Comforting Place

*It is not often that two 11-year-olds get to lead worship. This Sunday our thoughts turned to those with mental illnesses. We invited Rachel and Samantha to lead a discussion based on the recently released* Harry Potter and the Prisoner of Azkaban *film, whose graphic 'dementors' filled even adults with dread. In Rachel's words: 'A dementor is a "soul-stealer" that feeds on a victim's happy memories ultimately sucking out the soul leaving only an empty shell.' Christ's invitation to table is here seen as an invitation to rest.*

Jesus is here
The Spirit is with us!

So, it is Jesus who invites you, not me
To gather around this table
As you have gathered so many
    times before
As you have never gathered before.

Come
Not because I invite you
Come
Not because you want to
Come

For this is your home
This is the comforting place
Where Jesus meets
not saints
but sinners
not heroes
but ordinary people
made extraordinary
by the creative love of God.

Come
Gather
Bring your doubts and your fears
Bring your nightmares
Bring your failures
And lay them all
at the foot of the cross.

When the darkness threatens
to overwhelm
when tiredness beckons you
temptingly
to sink into despair
when the voices of hopelessness
challenge your faith.

Come
Gather
Be with your friends
Be with your family
Be with those who love you.

Be
With Christ.

Who,
on the night when chaos reigned
when powerful voices were raised against him
when friends deserted and betrayed him
when dark forces swirled all around him
took the time to be with friends.
He took a piece of bread
and lovingly shared it with them.
Take
eat
This is my body, shared with you.

When the meal was ended
he took the cup
and blessed it to them
This cup is my promise
wherever you go
my love will go with you.

For neither death
nor life
nor powers
nor principalities
nor things living
nor things dead
nor fears real
nor threats imagined
can separate you from the love of God.

So take the bread
and drink the wine
Remember Christ's presence
and celebrate God's love.

Peace-maker
Calm-bringer
God-with-us

You have emptied us
of all that frightens us
and holds us back

You have filled us
with your love
and your peace

So send us out into the world
To spread peace
To bring calm
and to share your creative love
with all and with each other.

# Why Are We Here?

*Clare and I never argue! Much. This prayer was written for a service where Clare and I 'dialogued' – argued – instead of having a sermon, playing with our differences and attempting some greater understanding through holding the differences together.*

Why are we here?
We are here to meet the unmeetable God.
Unknowable, made known in human life.
Eternal, crucified
Life, in broken bread and spilled wine.
Acceptance, in judgement and realism.
Love.

Who are we?
We are everyone. We are no one.
Male, female
Young, old
Black, white
Rich, poor.
Lost in the crowd
Accepted and loved

Where do we meet?
We meet in a much-loved building.
We meet in a run-down inner city hall.
We meet in a third-world shanty.
We meet in a glorious cathedral.
We meet in a factory,
in a post office queue.
We meet in Openshaw.
We meet in Iraq.

How do we worship?
How can we give praise to the unknowable mystery?
And still we meet...

46

# The Saints of God

*Clare lives in one of the oldest houses in Openshaw which was built as part of the farm on whose land the area was built. She even looks out on the local park, which is about as close to a green as we get! Nevertheless, if Delamere Park has seen a shepherdess in the last two hundred years, I would be amazed! Yet this old hymn— which we know from the old* Baptist Hymn Book *(1962)— says something important about who the true saints of God are. It is usually sung to the tune Grand Isle. I can't remember whether the nun in our version was one of the local sisters, one of our friends from El Salvador or a rhyming device. I don't think it matters too much!*

1. I sing a song of the saints of God,
   Patient and brave and true;
   Who toiled and fought and lived and died,
   For the Lord they loved and knew.
   And one was homeless, and one was old,
   And one was a traveller in the cold:
   And with God by my side all the way I'll be bold,
   For I mean to be one too.

2. They loved their Lord, who gave his life,
   And his love made them strong;
   And to follow his way was their delight,
   Though they sometimes got it wrong.
   And one was a minister, and one was a nun,
   And one was a child whose life was just begun:
   And with Christ before, the race I'll run
   For I mean to be one too.

3. They lived not only in ages past,
   There are hundreds and thousands still;
   Though the road may be rough and the workers few,
   Who seek to do Jesus' will.
   Yet still they are here and they urge us on,
   Whether young or old, whether here or gone:
   For the saints of God look like you and like me
   And I mean to be one too.

# The Tree of our Hopes

*Advent is a time of waiting, of expectation, the last few months of pregnancy when birth is inevitable but cannot be hurried. The beginning of this eucharist, with its exaggerated punctuation, is an attempt to take a deep breath and slow down. To savour the waiting. This is the time. This is the place. In this particular year we decided to make a Jesse Tree and found last year's Christmas tree languishing in Tim and Deborah's back yard, hanging onto life despite many yellowy brownish needles. The idea of an almost dead tree seemed to reflect something of our hopes and dreams – hanging on for dear life. Gradually, as Christmas drew near, the tree came to life with the glittery decorated pictures that the children had made, a sparkly testimony to the beauty of a dead tree and the struggle for life.*

Stop. Wait awhile. Savour the moment.
Stop. Wait awhile. Enjoy the here and now.
Stop. Wait awhile. You don't have to go.
Pause. Rest. Be.
For this is the time. And this is the place.
Not the time for anything. Not the place where anything happens.
This is the time. This is the place. And these are the people.
Stop. Wait awhile.

Stop. Wait awhile and give thanks.
Give thanks for this moment, for this space,
Give thanks for the people around us,
the people who are part of us,
the people who make us who we are,
the people who give us life.
Give thanks for the people who make us weep,
the people who make us angry,
the people who bring out the worst in us,
the people who bring out the best in us,
the people who make us calm,
the people who bring us joy,
the people who give us life,
the people who make us who we are,
the people who are part of us.
Give thanks for the people around us,
Give thanks for this moment, this space.
Stop. Wait awhile and give thanks.

*The tree of our hopes*

      *stands withered and dry*

    *gnarled and broken*

*dead*

     *to the touch*

*dead*

     *to the future*

    *dead*

*The tree of our hopes*

      *stands withered and dry*

    *and with it*

*our past*

     *has come to a halt*

    *futile*

    *spent*

   *dead*

So place your pictures on the tree:
the tree which bears our hopes
the tree which carries our story
the tree which conveys our dreams
the tree which
in its death
becomes our life
and in its past
becomes the future of the world.

So nail your memory on the tree:
the tree which bears our hopes
the tree which carries our story
the tree which conveys our dreams
the tree which
in its death
becomes our life
and in its past
becomes the future of the world.

Take, eat, this is my body broken for you.
Do this in memory of me.

Take, drink of my life-blood,
and be one.

We have tasted the first fruits
We have tasted new life
We have tasted resurrection
Send us out to tend new life
in this our community
and to the ends of the Earth

help other people

things

Love each

say "Thankyou"

say "please"

# Thanksgiving
## How Can We Sing Our Songs?

One year a visitor joined us for Remembrance Sunday, a service which means a lot to our community, when old people who have lived through war can share their memories and stories and unite in pledging themselves to live for peace with children who have not yet learned to grieve. The service probably began a few minutes after eleven o'clock with two minutes of almost silence, interrupted only by the noise of children trying hard to remain quiet. Our friend coped well with this. His tolerance was, however, stretched to the limit a few moments later as we sang Abide With Me. Exhausted by the effort of staying still for so long, the children decided that this great hymn of faith was the perfect occasion to dance!

How can we sing our songs? How can we dance in the midst of so much pain?

Imogen and Beth are here dressed as poppies on which are written the things they thought they could do to make life more peaceful.
We remember
We confess
We sing our songs
We pledge ourselves...

# How Can We?

How can we break bread
    and not remember those
      who have no bread?

How can we meet together
    and not remember those
      separated from their families
      and friends?

How can we shelter here
    and not remember those
      whose only shelter is a refugee camp
      or cardboard box?

How can we speak of peace
    and not remember those
      whose peace is shattered by constant
      fear and the rattle of guns?

How can we sing our hymns
    and not remember those
      who cannot openly express
      their religious beliefs?

How can we offer our gifts
    and not remember those
      who are caught in the never-ending cycle
      of poverty and debt?

How can we pour wine
    and not remember those
      who are imprisoned by addiction to
      bottle, needles or pills?

How can we celebrate
    and not remember those
      who suffer from depression,
      mental illness or grief?

God of human experience
    born in a stable in Bethlehem
      Spirit alive in us today

In our breaking of bread and pouring of wine,
    may we look outwards to the
    suffering of our world
      remembering the hope of your Shalom.

# Celebrating the Sacred in the Pain

## Prayers for a New Year

*Yet another year has passed. The children have put away their stockings (except our family custom dictates that our Christmas decorations stay up until twelfth night). Time to turn our attention to the possibilities of the year ahead. We have celebrated the miracle of the incarnation, the hope of new life in the midst of a cold, dark winter. The time to celebrate is now, the time to mourn is now, the time to believe there is hope is now ... and so we break bread together.*

VOICE 1: AMEN
VOICE 2: For ever
VOICE 3: And ever
VOICE 4: TOCK
VOICE 5: Tick
VOICE 6: Tick, Tock; Tick Tock
VOICE 7: As it was in the beginning,
is now and ever shall be.

VOICE 1: The beginning
VOICE 2: The end
VOICE 1: All our yesterdays
VOICE 2: All our tomorrows
VOICE 7: As it was in the beginning,
is now and ever shall be.

VOICE 3: Carpe Diem
VOICE 4: Seize the day
VOICE 5: Give up yourself unto this moment
VOICE 6: The time is now
VOICE 7: As it was in the beginning,
is now and ever shall be.

VOICE 1:  Born
VOICE 2:  In blood and water
VOICE 1:  Born
VOICE 2:  In stable and sin
VOICE 6:  The time is now
VOICE 3:  Carpe Diem
VOICE 1:  Born
VOICE 5:  A baby!
VOICE 4:  A God!
VOICE 1:  Born
VOICE 7:  As it was in the beginning,
              is now and ever shall be.

VOICE 3:  A moment seized
VOICE 4:  A life lived
VOICE 3:  A moment seized
VOICE 4:  Life in all its fullness
VOICE 7:  I am come that you might have life
VOICE 5:  Know Life

VOICE 6:  No Life
VOICE 2:  Abused
VOICE 3:  Tortured
VOICE 2:  Forgotten
VOICE 3:  Denied
VOICE 6:  No Life
VOICE 1:  No hope
VOICE 2:  No future
VOICE 1:  Eternity stops
VOICE 2:  The End

VOICE 7:  As it was in the beginning,
              is now and ever shall be.

VOICE 1:  Bread broken
VOICE 3:  Body given, hope ended.

VOICE 2:  Wine poured
VOICE 4:  Blood shed, promise sealed.

VOICE 7:  As it was in the beginning,
              is now and ever shall be.

VOICE 6:  Tock, tick; tock, tick.
VOICE 5:  Tick
VOICE 4:  TOCK
VOICE 3:  Ever
VOICE 2:  And for ever
VOICE 1:  AMEN

# Journey to the Cross

*These three calls to worship trace Jesus' 'Holy Week' journey, from the triumphal entry of Palm Sunday, through Maundy Thursday in Bethany to the cross of Good Friday.*
*Salvadoran theologian Jon Sobrino has contrasted 'celebration', with 'entertainment'. In the affluent north of the planet, our temptation is to look for entertainment, demanding ever bigger and better TV sets, sitting passively while 'performers' provide our amusement. The poor, he maintains, know how to celebrate. In their struggle for survival and justice, they are active participants. Their worship is a true celebration.*
*ESOL is educational jargon: English for Speakers of Other Languages.*

Jesus calls us to journey with him,
to journey with him in the celebration of arriving at the city's gates,
to journey with him in the rhythm of a donkey's stride,
to journey with him in the celebration of the carnival procession.

Jesus calls us to party with him,
to party with him in the end of year awards ceremony of an ESOL class,
to party with him in the carnival floats and samba dancers of the city centre,
to party with him in the marquees and stalls of a celebration of community.

**And Jesus calls us to celebrate in the joyful sounds of play,**
**to celebrate the rebuilding of shattered lives,**
**to celebrate the acceptance of difference and diversity,**
**to celebrate the reconciliation of divided communities.**

Jesus calls us to journey with him,
to journey with him to a woman pouring perfume in a house at Bethany,
to journey with him to a man pouring water, cleaning up after the devastation of war,
to journey with him to a woman pouring lotion on the bruises of a husband's violence.

Jesus calls us to speak out with him,
to speak out for the beauty of a woman's extravagance,
to speak out for the unveiling of rules that deny people's existence,
to speak out for justice for the poorest of the poor.

**And Jesus calls us to celebrate in the dance of liberation,
to celebrate love wherever it is found,
to celebrate the many gifts offered by women and men,
to celebrate the dignity and worth of all people.**

Jesus calls us to journey with him,
to journey with him in a last meal shared with friends in an upper room,
to journey with him in the turmoil of a garden in Gethsemane,
to journey with him in the grief of those stood at the foot of a cross.

Jesus calls us to keep vigil with him,
to keep vigil with him in the waiting for news of an abducted teenager,
to keep vigil with him in the uncertainty of a wire cage in Guantánamo Bay,
to keep vigil with him in the hospital room of the latest victim of gang-land violence.

And Jesus calls us to celebrate in the holding on to hope,
to celebrate the restoration of  justice,
to celebrate the freedom of political expression,
to celebrate the healing of all who are oppressed.

# Footprints

*One of the stories our older folk love to tell is of the old Whit Walks, each church proudly walking behind its banner along the tarmac and cobbles of our familiar terraced streets.*
*This eucharist picks up both the theme of journeying and the theme of the cost of following Jesus. Our journey takes us to the foot of the cross. It is not a comfortable journey. But it is a journey trodden by countless others before us, from the famous Martin Luther King to those we know of in our own communities. Here, we name the saints of our own community but these should be changed to reflect a different congregation or events in your local news. The cross, painful though it is, is not the end of the journey...*

Footprints, some large, some tiny,
some straight, some winding,
some lightly trodden,
others heavy,
as if they carry the world on their backs,
imprint their journey across the face of the earth
to the foot of the cross.

Here footprints criss cross their journeys
some racing on by, some glancing around,
some paused in contemplation
others rooted in horror
what little innocence there was
lost stumbling and tripping along the way
to the foot of the cross.

'Come, take up your cross and follow me.'

And we count the cost in our own lives and
    in those who journey with us
in the stories told by our footprints
imprinted on the earth,
times of happiness, banners held high,
times of grief, the procession slow,
travelling with us or travelling alone,
to the foot of the cross.

'Come, take up your cross and follow me.'

And we look up at the cross
and we look out at the world which is our home
and we count the cost of following
the path of peace and justice
imprinted in your footprints
imprinted in the lives of those who've
    gone before
to the foot of the cross.

And we think of Martin Luther King
and Rosa Parks,
Mahatma Gandhi
and Oscar Romero,
Mother Teresa
and the woman named on the local news
as the Good Samaritan of Salford
And we think of Tim Clay
and Margaret and Marjorie,
and the countless others whose stories
    we can tell
and the countless others whose stories
    are known only to others.
And we stand in mourning and solidarity
with the community of Beslan, Russia
in their loss of 330 killed in the school siege,
nailed in your body on the cross.

For it is here that our footprints lead us,
here to the foot of the cross,
not to escape the violence of our world,
but to acknowledge our own and humanity's sin.
And it is here that you raise our faces to look
    at you
and offer us hope, dare us to dream,
of a restored, resurrected world.

For it is here that our footprints lead us,
here to the foot of the cross,
for it is here you invite us to feast
here you invite us to celebrate
here you invite us to live out our dreams
to write the stories of our recreated lives
to write the stories of our resurrected world.

This is my body,
the bread of earth,
made by human hands,
the bread of heaven,
ripped apart by human hands,
This is my body, broken for you,
Do this in memory of me.

This is my blood,
the wine of earth,
celebration of life,
the wine of heaven,
celebration of all that humanity can be,
This is my blood, poured out for you,
Do this in memory of me.

And so our footprints are joined together
at the foot of the cross,
Here we have confessed and been set free,
Here we have feasted and celebrated.
Here we continue our journeys
and invite others to join us
to walk your path of justice and of peace.

# Seeing through Your Eyes

Dear God
We sit here
this morning
in your presence
You
the creator
You
the life
You
are here
with us
in us
around us

And we can't see you.

We look for a king
We look for someone special
We look for fame and fortune

And we can't see you.

We look for power and glory
We look for beauty
We look for celebrity

And we can't see you.

We can see a beautiful old man
We can see a laughing child
We can see a loving parent

But we can't see you.

We can see a faithful follower
We can see a generous friend
We can see a caring relative

But we can't see you.

Forgive us Jesus
when we fall into the trap
of seeing things
through the world's eyes

We look for a king
and find a carpenter on a donkey

Help us to see through your eyes.

# 'Stupid Northerners' and 'Foolish Women'

*Before the letters of complaint arrive, let me point out that it was me (Tim) who wrote this call to worship. I am a 'stupid northerner'. When I was at university I even owned a flat cap – and when I was growing up, there was a man across the road from me who genuinely did keep whippets! Clare, the posh southerner, is a 'foolish woman'. Stereotypes are there to be subverted.*
*Sophisticated Jerusalemites would not have expected their king to come from Galilee. Kings don't ride donkeys.*

The branches are cut
Our cloaks laid out
We're waiting for the king.
Expectant hush
of awed respect
The crowds are murmuring.
Where's the king?
I can't see
Stand still and stop pushing.

Who's this bloke in the road?
Where's the chariot?
Where's the army?
All there is is a donkey,
a few foolish women,
and some stupid northerners.

We're waiting for the king
Expectant hush
of awed respect
The crowds are murmuring.
Where's the king?
I can't see
Stand still and stop pushing.

# In the Middle of the Darkest Night

In the middle of the darkest night
when I'm lying wide awake
tossing and turning
trying to get comfy
**You are there**

When I have to try something new
and I'm frightened of failing
afraid of looking silly
scared of myself
**You are there**

When the pain seems overwhelming
when I feel I can't go on
when the sadness fills my heart
and thunder rages in my head
**You are there**

You are with me in the good times
You are with me in the bad times
You are there when I am happy
You are there when I am sad

You are there when I am good
You are there when I am naughty
You are there when I feel kind
You are there when I feel cross

So we meet this morning to say thank you
Thank you for being with us
Thank you for being our friend
Thank you for loving us
whatever we do
wherever we go
whoever we are

61

# Eucharist for an Autumn Equinox

*This eucharist could also have been called 'Ode to a Tree' as it was inspired by a single tree in a blaze of autumn colour, half obscured by advertising hoardings and boarded up houses. It is not often that we take time to stop and contemplate a particular tree or even to reflect on the passing of the seasons that give our lives rhythm and a sense of moving on.*

It stands there
not particularly tall
or shouting for attention
but crowned
in the magnificent beauty
of autumn splendour
Warm russets
golden ochres
rich magentas
adorn branches
laden with the
ripened seeds
that hold the promise
of generations
who are yet to be
an orgasmic finale
to summer's
laid back symphony
the orchestra
ebbing and flowing
to mark summer's passing
in a blaze of glory.

Around the city
the tree stands
largely unnoticed
masked by the
hustle and bustle
of supermarket
and benefit queues
hidden by the
shabbiness of
boarded up houses
and the glinting
of broken glass
eclipsed by
the plastic wrapped
bouquets of flowers
tied ceremoniously
to the iron railings
of busy road junctions
and as the nights draw in
the rain drops begin to trickle
like leaves as tears fall
to mourn the passing of time.

For autumn is a season
of sharp contradictions
of mellow fruitfulness
where our canned harvests
are gathered in and given out
a time of great beauty
where wisdom gained
through maturity
savours the fullness of being
and celebrates
our treasured achievements
But autumn too
marks the time for pruning
for cutting back
and taking stock
the stripping away
as we burrow once again
into the darkness
of the blessing place
where our spirits
shape their stories
and our souls keep vigil.

Here, where the soul resides
we gather around the table
a vision of community
the dream of Shalom
a glimpse of glory
the place where we
re-enact our trust
in the rhythms of life
that pulsate within us
For this is the place
where heaven touches earth
where we re-tell the story
that has shaped our lives
It is here that we grieve for
    the violence
that is in us and around us
it is here we learn to live with
    pain and loss
This is my body, this is my
    blood
It is here that we celebrate
    the possibility
that life can grow out of death
it is here we celebrate hope
for restored community
The bread of heaven, the wine
    of new life.

So as we gather
to tell the story
of a particular life
that is part of all our lives
we too create the space
to begin to share our stories
what has gone before
who we are now
our dreams for the future
and as autumn reminds us
time cycles into eternity
the rhythms of life
ebbing and flowing
in the routines of our days
and the dreams of our nights
who we are
and who we are yet to be
held by one another
in the vulnerability of
    community
held by the one
who is yesterday, today
and for ever.

# Faces of God

*This two-voiced eucharist began life as a reflection contrasting the 'unknowability' and distance of God as portrayed in W. Chalmers Smith's well known hymn Immortal, Invisible, God Only Wise and in the fourteenth-century classic of Christian spirituality The Cloud of Unknowing with the God spoken of in Isaiah 66.10-14. In contrast the God of Isaiah 66 is pictured as a mother, nursing her children at her breast, cradling us in her arms and bouncing us on her knees. Here God is intimate, God is physical and dare I say it, sexual. It is this intimate, knowable God that is made known to us in the city, in the everyday reality of our lives and yet is not confined to our own limited understandings of God.*

God who is beyond knowing,
God who is beyond the bounds of
    human language
God who is completely other
Distanced from humanity
Immortal
Invisible
Only wise.

> *God who exists in birthing life*
> *God who suckles a child at her breast*
> *God who is intimate*
> *One with humanity*
> *Mortal*
> *Visible*
> *Foolish.*

*God who is made known in the city*
*God who is incarnate in the bored youths*
*and beggars*
*God who is intimate*
*One with humanity*
*Mortal*
*Visible*
*Foolish.*

> God who cannot suffer
> God who cannot change or be changed
> God who is completely other
> Distanced from humanity
> Impassable
> Immutable
> Knowing all.

God who exists not in physical form
God who exists not in earthly shape or
    human guise
God who is completely other
Distanced from humanity
Immortal
Invisible
Only wise.

> *God who hangs on a cross*
> *God who is challenged and changed*
> *God who is intimate*
> *One with humanity*
> *Passionate*
> *Changeable*
> *Vulnerable.*

God who is beyond need
God who is beyond emotion or passion
God who is completely other
Distanced from humanity
Impassable
Immutable
Knowing all.

*God who breaks bread with the hungry*
*God who shares wine forging relationships*
*God who is intimate*
*One with humanity*
*Passionate*
*Changeable*
*Vulnerable.*

For God is made known to us
in this most holy of sacraments.

*For God is made known to us*
*in these most down-to-earth elements.*

God is made known to us
in the breaking of bread
and pouring of wine.

God is made known to us
in our sharing of bread
and sharing of wine.

This is my body.
This is my blood.

Do this in memory of me.
Do this in memory of us.

God who contradicts our systems and
    categories

*God who confounds our expectations*

God who confuses our neat understandings

*Bone of our bone*

Flesh of our flesh

*Made known in bread and wine*

Made known in the depths of human
    experience

Made known in our love for each other.

# Humble God

*Right-on, urban trendies sometimes appreciate a bit of rural tranquillity, too! For many years, on Christmas Eve, a group of friends and acquaintances would gather to celebrate 'Midnight Mass' in a stable with Donny, the horse and his companion goats Cedric and Jenny. People would perch on straw bales and a doll – or when Beth and Imogen were newborn, a real baby! – was placed into a real manger. The wine was rarely 'poured' because for some reason it usually worked out that no one had remembered to bring a goblet. So the bottle was passed around! On one famous occasion, the eucharistic wine, after being shared, was placed on the floor by the manger, only to be knocked over by a very excited Kimmy, the sheepdog.*
*Silent night, holy night.*

Humble God,
born into the shabbiness
of an unlit stable,
**we glimpsed your glory then**
**amid the dirt and din**
**of domesticated animals,**
**amid the blood and toil**
**of human birth.**

Humble God,
living among the poverty
of simple, down-to-earth folk,
**we glimpsed your glory then**
**in meeting and touching**
**the outcasts and untouchables,**
**in sharing bread, wine and stories**
**with women and sinners.**

Humble God,
dying in the pain
of a torturer's cross,
**we glimpsed your glory then**
**in speaking kind words**
**with common criminals,**
**in concern and forgiveness**
**for those who had put him to death.**

Humble God,
rising in the quiet
of a garden tomb,
**we glimpsed your glory then**
**in the emptiness of the tomb,**
**'He is not here! He is risen!'**
**in the astonishment and disbelief**
**as women run to tell the story,**
**and Peter goes home amazed.**

Humble God,
risen with us now
in the fragile miracles of human life,
**we glimpse your glory now**
**in the love, laughter and beauty**
**we share with one another,**
**in the depths of humanity**
**as we respond to the needs and suffering**
**of our world.**

# Words into the Silence

*Listen to the voice of God, we optimistically instruct believers. Listen. The Word spoke. And there was. At the beginning of the third millennium, the words we hear are war, famine, unemployment, terrorism, dictatorship, poverty, disease. Few people claim, Joan of Arc-like, literally to hear the voice of God. We cry out in distress and are answered with silence. God is silent. God is silence. We speak our words into God's silence. Words into silence. Human words transformed into God's silence, God's silence transformed into the Creative Word who was with God in the beginning.*

In the beginning
was the Word
In the beginning
was the Silence
out of which the Word was spoken.

Be still
and know
that God is.

In the middle
was the Word
In the middle
we tried
to express our faith
in words
which reflected your glory.

Be still
and know
that God is.

Know that God is
Believe that God is
Trust that God is.

Do not try to tie God down
with your words
with your formulae
with your cleverness.

Listen
to the Silence
Listen
to the Silence
Listen
to God.

And in the end
will be the Word
And in the end
will be the Silence
out of which the eternal Word
will speak.

# The Unseen God

*Joel is at that age where he has realized that when we ask him questions in church, the answer is always going to be either 'God' or 'Jesus'. He is very competitive and always tries to be the first to put his hand up and call out the answer. Another of his favourite answers is 'Everywhere.' As in, where do we see God? Everywhere. This is particularly important for a tiny, fragile congregation worshipping in a run down old chapel in the middle of a deprived community which is about to be torn down. Where do we see God? Everywhere.*

The unseen God calls us together
The unseen God calls us to meet
The unseen God calls us to greet
one another
the world
himself
herself
everywhere
nowhere
here
there
now
then

then
in the story of a journey
then
in the journey of a people
then
in people who brought us
to where we are today

now
in the people who love us
now

in the love we share
there
with all of creation
here
with one another

For we remember the events
of one dark night
when love was murdered
and hope died
We remember the events
of arrest and betrayal
when God was unseen
and justice was hidden

We remember the meal
when love was shared
'This is my body, broken for you'
Love which could not die

We remember the meal
when hope was shared
'This cup is the new promise,
        sealed with my blood'

As we share bread and wine
As we share Christ's body and blood
we share love
we share hope
with one another
with all creation
and with God

Unseen God
we have seen your face
we have feasted with you
as we share with one another
Send us out
to make you known
to proclaim that there is hope
and to share your love

# Blessings

*Just occasionally we leave church with a feeling of having encountered the living, celebrating, dancing God. Such an encounter sends us out humming the final hymn, tapping our toes – or even, in Imogen's case, whirling like a Dervish and dressed like a ballerina! The first of these blessings was co-written with Jill Thornton.*

Let us go from here
Held in the knowledge that we are beautifully made
in the image of God
Strengthened by knowing that the brokenness of Christ
reflects the fragmentation of our lives
And empowered by the knowledge that through the Spirit
we are called to reflect the image of God in our world

> May the blessing of the extravagant God
> whose Spirit encourages us
> to see our own self-worth
> be with us all
> and with all people
> silenced by violence or abuse
> empowering us with the knowledge
> that we are all beautifully made in your image

May the music of life
play on in our heads
like the nagging, unforgettable tune.
May the music of life
play on in our hearts
like the rhythm of life itself.
May the music of life
play on in our spirits
leading us on in the dance
Now and for ever.

# Spinning Dreams

*In the beginning, there is a future.*
*Like the circle into which our dreams are woven, life, history, story comes and goes, round and round.*
*In the beginning, there is a future.*

Dream-catcher Spirit,
Long ago you spun the universe into being,
spun the glinting sun and the glistening moon,
spun the earth in its myriad of textures and colours,
spun a planet teeming with life and diversity.

Dream-catcher Spirit,
You continue to spin through the universe,
spinning the changing landscape of the earth,
spinning the miracle of each human birth,
spinning yourself into the fabric of our lives.

Dream-catcher Spirit,
You catch the bitterness of dreams used to harm,
catch our acts of oppression and destruction,
catch our indifference to the suffering of earth's children,
holding in yourself our brokenness and vulnerability.

Dream-catcher Spirit,
Spin in us your dreams of life lived in all its fullness,
Spin in us your hopes of harmony and peace,
Spin in us your challenge to live in community,
Spin with us lives honouring the beauty of earth.

# Narrative: The Story

## Autumn Thanksgiving

*Each year I half dread the coming of autumn, the drawing in of the nights, the misty mornings when you can see your breath hanging on the air. Yet it is also a season of great beauty, a time of preparation for the lean times ahead, a time for reflection, enticing us towards the end of the year.*
*I once led a service where I attempted to explain communion to three- and four-year-olds. It was autumn and so we used the example of chestnuts falling from the trees, lying uried in the ground ready to rise again in the spring. The children had no difficulty in making the connection between the chestnuts lying buried in the ground and the death and resurrection of Jesus.*

God of the autumn mists
and winter frosts,

We give you thanks...
for the continuing cycle of life;
for the drawing in of autumn
and the letting go of winter,
for the closing of another year
and preparing for the next.

We give you thanks...
for a life lived to the full;
lived in service and love for others,
lived in challenging injustice,
for a life so tragically destroyed,
an attempt to silence the pulse of life.

We give you thanks...
that the story doesn't end here;
that the icy grip of winter,
doesn't have the last word.
We look in hope for the promise of spring
and the birthing of new life.

# Advent Litany

*It is very easy to be sentimental about Christmas. The nativity is displayed with shiny colourful figurines cast from plaster with holy fixed expressions on their faces. There may be real straw but it is clean and sweet smelling. And the baby never cries! On one occasion while abroad, we visited a grotto fenced off as a permanent nativity shrine. I tried hard not to smile as I noticed that Mary had lost a plaster hand, Joseph's staff stood at half mast and the baby Jesus had a grubby face!*
*This litany attempts to bring a dose of reality to our Christmas nativity scenes and to relate the incarnation to our less than perfect world.*

Voice 1:    Marginalized God
Born in a cattle stall, laid in a feeding trough,
Born of a teenager, your parentage questioned.

Voice 2:    We remember today all those who struggle to bring up children:
the single father whose benefit is to be cut
the pregnant teenager looking for support not condemnation
the overworked mother juggling a career and family life

All:    **Marginalized God**
**You shake us from the centre of our cosy world**
**Calling us to the starkness of a cattle stall**

Voice 1:    Marginalized God
Born in a strange town, far from home,
Born out of pain, into the labour of human life.

Voice 2:    We remember today all those who have no home:
the child living on a pavement abused by those who were supposed to care
a middle-aged couple fleeing to the safety of a refugee camp
an elderly man facing deportation away from his family

All:    **Marginalized God**
**You shake us from the centre of our cosy world**
**Calling us to the starkness of a cattle stall**

Voice 1:    Marginalized God
Fleeing from Herod, warned by a dream,
Fleeing from bloodshed, to the violence of the cross.

Voice 2:    We remember today all those who live in fear of violence:
the political prisoner waiting for the next round of questions and beatings
the elderly woman too frightened to go out at night
the woman scared to go home never knowing what mood he will be in

**All:**    **Marginalized God**
**You shake us from the centre of our cosy world**
**Calling us to the starkness of a cattle stall**

Voice 1:    Marginalized God
Visited by shepherds, and by eastern astronomers,
Humanity and divinity touch in the miracle of birth.

Voice 2:    We celebrate today with all those whose lives offer new signs of hope:
the middle-aged man who has been reunited with his family
the woman who has returned home after being evacuated
the grandparent who holds his new grandchild for the first time

**All:**    **Marginalized God**
**In you humanity and divinity touch**
**Birth in us your hope for the world**

# The Silent God

*The First World War shattered the liberal optimism and hope of the nineteenth century. Church attendances and belief in God have been in decline ever since. Humanity cries out to God in distress. Humanity cries out to God, begging for relief. God does not answer. Innocent children are born into poverty and starve to death without ever enjoying the riches of God's creation. Auschwitz; Rwanda; El Salvador; Srebrenitza... God does not answer. Yet still we pray. We need to listen very hard to hear the sound of a Creator in the midst of so many cries, so much human noise pollution. And still we pray. And still we pray...*

Shhhh!
Be quiet.
Be very, very quiet.

Listen to the sound of your heartbeat.
Listen to the noise of the cars.
Listen to the wind, rustling the leaves.
Listen to the rain on the roof.

Be still
and know
that God is

In the beginning
Before God spoke
Before the breath of God swept across the
    waters
Before everything

There was silence.

Shhhh!
Be quiet.
Be very, very quiet.

Listen to the sound of God
Listen to the silence
out of which God speaks
out of which God calls.

Come to me
Come and hear again
My Word
My Story
My Name

Come and hear my creative power,
giving birth to all that is.
Come and hear my loving law
guiding your daily life.
Come and hear my prophetic judgement
calling you to repent.
Come and hear my dying cry
forgiving you your folly.
Come and hear my challenging summons
calling you to build Shalom.

Come to each other
Come and share again
Your words
Your stories
Your names

Come
Gather
Share

Share bread
made in creation
broken in remembrance
Share wine
made in heaven
spilled in forgetfulness

On the night before the Word of God was
    silenced
Jesus gathered his friends around him
In the midst of raucous celebration
He paused
Bread broken
Wine shared
This is my body
This is my blood
And darkness covered the earth
And there was silence

After three days of silence
birdsong woke the dawn
with a song
which we still share today

God who is silent,
God who speaks
You have filled the silence of our hearts
with the promise of your eternal Word.
Help us to hear your silence
and to know your voice.
Send us out
to sing your song
and live your word,
now and for evermore.

# Remembrance Confession

*When we look back and remember friends, family and strangers who have died in war, the last thing we want is to be startled, confused or challenged by linguistic playfulness. We stand. We remember. We confess.*

God who is peace,
We stand by,
allowing our
governments
to proclaim war –
on terrorism,
on countries
whose leaders
we dislike,
on drugs,
on crime.

God who is peace,
We buy food
produced
by exploited labour,
goods crafted
by children,
financial products
profiting from
arms sales
and environmental
destruction.

God who is peace,
forgive us
for our silence
and complicity,
for our living as
part of an unjust
    system.
Help us
to forgive ourselves,
to know when
we have done
all we can
and give us peace.

# Eucharist for Remembrance Sunday

*Every year, Ida buys a new wreath which she lays on our war memorial. Until the last couple of years, the old wreath was always taken with honour and dignity to the Cenotaph. Military service and the experience of war have changed the lives of so many in our world and our community. To remember fallen loved ones, to commit oneself to strive for peace and to stand for two minutes in silent repentance for our part in the sinful structures of the world is not to glory in triumphal militarism but to re-member, to put our lives back together. Read rhythmically, this 'mantra' echoes the rhythm of life and death.*

As this bread was once grain
scattered on the hillside
so you have brought us together
to share in one loaf
to eat of one body

The body of Christ lies broken in the ground
The body of Christ lies forgotten in the ground

For there is no resurrection
while the dead are forgotten
There is no resurrection
while love fades and dies

The body of Christ is dismembered
    ripped apart
The body of Christ is broken ripped apart

There is no resurrection
while politicians send children to die
There is no resurrection
while widows mourn

The body of Christ is mutilated, defaced
The body of Christ is broken, defaced

For there is no resurrection
while churches exclude and religion divides
There is no resurrection
while people claim God in their own image

For on the night when he was betrayed
Jesus gathered with his friends
with tax collectors and prostitutes
with fishermen and revolutionaries
with friends and betrayers
They shared the goodness of the earth
and ate a meal together

Together they ate
Together they shared

This is my body
This is my body broken
This is my body broken for you

Take it
eat it

remember
remember me
re-member me

remember the broken ones
remember the excluded
remember the dead
remember the loveless
remember those whom you despise

Together they drank
Together they shared

This is my blood shed
blood shed
bloodshed

poured out for all humanity
poured out with all humanity

My blood
Your blood
Our blood mingled

the promise of peace
the promise of new life
the promise of resurrection
the promise of Shalom
the promise of eternal life together

God of life and death
We have looked back and remembered
And in our remembering we look forward
to your wholeness
to your healing
to your Shalom
In your death we find life
In your brokenness we find wholeness
In your past we find the future of all that is
Send us out in your Spirit
Send us out to remember
Send us out to re-member

# The Swirling Whirling Waters

*It is often said that one in four adults will suffer from a mental illness at some time during their lives. This includes Christians. This includes ministers. Mental illness is an ever-present reality. Can we reflect this in our worship? Can the creative God understand depression?*

The waters move over the face of the earth
The deep
dark
waters
The waters
The swirling, whirling waters
Currents Tides Eddies Flows
Mysterious, threatening waters, hiding their power
beneath their beauty
Breaking Destroying Breaking
Swamping
Surging Breaking
Breaking
Waves Breakers Swelling Breaking
The waters pull us down into the depths
Power unleashed to destroy and to kill
Overwhelming me

The Spirit moves over the face of the water
Gentle as a dove
Alighting where she wishes
Floating
Calmly
Over the seas
Beckoning

Come to me, all who are burdened
all who fear
Come to me
Come to me

78

On the night when the waters of despair threatened to overwhelm him, and when his friends would betray and abandon him, Jesus of Nazareth gathered them together in an upper room. Why are you afraid? Have you still no faith? He took a piece of bread, gave thanks, broke it and gave it to them. Why are you afraid? Have you still no faith? This is my body. I give it for you in love.

In the same way after supper, he took the cup and gave it to them saying, This cup is my eternal promise to be with you always. Peace, be still! Peace, be still!

God who is Mother and Father to us
God who is life and death to us
God, from whom all our blessings flow
We gather before you today
As we have done so many times before
As we have never done before
To praise the fountain of life

**Holy, holy, holy**
**God of mysterious power**
**God of wonderful vulnerability**
**The heavens sing your glory**
**The earth reflects your compassion**
**Hosanna in the highest**
**Blessed is the One who comes in your name**
**Hosanna in the highest**

In our fears, we see your protection
In our guilt, we see your forgiveness
In our self-loathing, we see your affirmation
And so, with all your people
with the saints and with our ancestors
with our sisters and brothers whom the spirit
    moves today
and with all who will breathe your life in days
    to come
We offer you our thanks and our praise
You who breathed life into the earth
You who hold back the waters of despair
You who measure the span of our life
You who walk among us
You who suffer with us
You who breathe hope into our future
You who knead us into a people

**For in eating of your body**
**We become community**

**In drinking your blood**
**We are a people of hope**

You have fed us with your body
And refreshed us with your blood
You have calmed the waves of our fears
And breathed your spirit of peace
And hope
Into our lives
And our future
Send us out to speak your Word into our world
Peace, Be Still!
        Peace, Be Still!

79

# Thunderbird Eucharist

*What is the bread we bring to the table? What does it represent? What is the wine that we so lovingly bring to our white clothed table? What does it symbolize? Are our bread and wine empty symbols, a ritual we re-enact because it is something we have always done, or do they represent the gritty, not too pretty realities of our lives and our world? Thunderbird is a very cheap, strong wine, whose sole merit is the ability to make the drinker very drunk very quickly. This is my body, this is my blood.*

Bring bread to the table;
*Bring the crust thrown to a starving child.*
Bring bread to the table;
*Bring the flour ground by exploited hands.*
Bring bread to the table;
*Bring the additives of human cleverness.*
Bring bread to the table;
*Bring the stale loaf bought by a*
    *desperate mother.*
Bring bread to the table;
*Bring the Body of Christ.*

Bring wine to the table;
*Bring the Saturday bottle, ground into*
*someone's face.*
Bring wine to the table;
*Bring Thunderbird, drunk in the morning.*
Bring wine to the table;
*Bring snobbery and pretentiousness.*
Bring wine to the table;
*Bring the bruises and hunger of a*
    *drunkard's family.*
Bring wine to the table;
*Bring the Blood of Christ.*

Holy God, we praise you.
Let the heavens be joyful
and let the earth be glad.

We bless you for creating the whole world,
for your promises to your people,
and for the human Jesus, in whose
    shining face,
we see your fullness.

Born of Mary, he shares our life.
In broken bread, he shares his life
*With the hungry,*
*With the exploited,*
*With the sick,*
*With the poor.*
In spilled wine, he shares his promise
*With the oppressed,*
*With the hopeless,*
*With the excluded,*
*With all the victims of this world.*

With thanksgiving we break the bread
And lift the cup.
We proclaim Christ's death and resurrection.
We claim the promise of life.

**Unite us in faith,**
**encourage us with hope,**
**inspire us to love,**
**that we may serve as your faithful disciples**
**until we join with all your people**
**around your banquet table.**

# A World Outside Your Window

*I remember the original Live Aid concerts and Bob Geldof in particular as he vented his righteous anger at the world's governments for standing by while Ethiopia starved on our TV screens. Geldof did not make comfortable viewing but he repeatedly stung the conscience of the world, 'where the only water flowing, is the bitter sting of tears...'. Here maybe, we have the widow's response to the inaction of the unjust judge of Luke 18.1–8.*

God of justice
We gather before you this morning
conscious of our own failings
conscious of the failings of the world
we have created
and which we fail to change.

God of justice
We gather before you this morning
in a world where money buys power
in a world where the needs of the poor
and the needs of the planet
are sacrificed to the demands of the market.
When will the Sabbath end
that we may buy and sell and make
    money again.
When will your Sabbath end?

God of justice
We gather before you this morning
and tremble
in fear.
We gather before you this morning
and wait
the verdict of your judgement.
We gather before you this morning
and wait.

God of justice
We gather before you this morning
and you do not judge us
We gather before you this morning

and in your mercy,
you do not hand down your verdict of
    condemnation.
We gather before you this morning
and you do not remain enthroned
on high
a judge, remote and unapproachable.

God of justice
We gather before you this morning
and your judgement comes to us
in your own life,
lived among us
one of us
showing us all that we can be
showing us all that we could be.

You judge us by your example
and in your love you summon us to new life
to new creation
to new justice.

God of justice
We gather before you this morning
and ask that our praise and our worship
    might lead us
into new commitment
and as such, we pledge ourselves
with your words.

**Our Father...**

# Narrative Eucharist

*The storyteller's art is one that has largely been lost in the West. TV programmes like* Jackanory *or* Story Makers *have re-introduced the idea of listening to a story, but that story is still fixed in a book. Here, Clare attempts to re-tell the Last Supper story as it might have been told before the printing press froze all our words.*

*It was written for one of our informal eucharistic meals around a kitchen table on a Saturday night. Depending on your tradition, you might want to use it at an Agape feast, or in a house group or other informal setting. Alternatively, it could be used with one person reading out the story while another mimes the actions. In our context, it would fit well in our informal Maundy Thursday liturgy.*

It is still dark. The women of the house have risen early, aware of the preparation a great feast such as the Passover requires. The younger girls, who have not yet reached womanhood, are sent out into the coolness of the breaking dawn to fetch water from the well in heavy earthenware jars. The old women occupy carved wooden benches near the newly lit oven and begin weaving their stories of lives lived, tales of great loves and tragic losses, to help while away the long hours of chopping and mixing, of kneading and baking. Young mothers feed babies, balancing them precariously on one hip, as they turn to the tasks of preparing a great meal. Toddlers play in the dirt of the kitchen floor, banging cooking utensils and pans in a manner to wake the whole neighbourhood.

As the heat of the sun rises through the narrow windows, the noise and bustle intensify. Voices are raised, laughter becomes more raucous, tears fall and arguments are resolved. And still the murmur of voices spinning their stories can be heard through the din of the pots boiling and children playing. The heat becomes almost unbearable as bowls full of dough are pummelled, stretched and kneaded, as arms and backs begin to ache and sweat trickles down tied-back hair. The smells mingle enticingly as the bread is shaped into rounds and makes its way to the oven. Soon the cooking and the baking are done and women and children perch, tired but elated, around the simple, homely kitchen, observing the fruits of their labours spilling out across the stone slab that serves as a kitchen table.

The men can be heard, low rough voices laughing and murmuring, occasionally raised in dissent, making their way back from the vineyards and olive groves, from the workshops and market places. The triumphs and disasters of the day are laughed about or lamented. Problems are mulled over and discussed as the sun loses its fire. The smell of damp earth and newly cut wood lingers on the gentleness of the evening breeze. The men's thoughts turn to the evening ahead, to enjoying the simple pleasures of food lovingly prepared; to sampling the fruits of hours of hard work in the vineyard and at the wine press; to meeting with distant family and old friends; to the giddiness of raucous music and the ripeness of female flesh on the dance floor.

As the men arrive, everyone pitches in to help transport the steaming food and yet-to-be-sampled wine a few dwellings down the dusty road, to an upper room especially prepared and decorated for the festivities. There is an atmosphere of great anticipation as the families, friends and neighbours prepare to welcome their friend and itinerant storyteller to the great feast. He is to take the place of honour at the centre of the table, to recite the incantations and perform the rituals that give the celebrations their sense of community history and meaning. The occasion is as solemn as it is celebratory, as sad as it is happy. Rumours have been rife in the town. Controversy cannot hide behind a simple life for long. Temple guards and Roman soldiers have made their presence felt. It is only a matter of time before something has to give.

'This is my body broken for you.' And the bread, so carefully and lovingly prepared, is ripped violently apart. There is a gasp and general feeling of dis-ease as the accepted protocol for the festival is put to one side and a new ritual is brought painfully to birth.

'This is my blood poured out for you.' And the wine, so skilfully and patiently brought to maturity, is poured brusquely into an earthenware cup. As we pass the cup from hand to hand around the room an uneasy silence rests over the gathering, aware that struggle and death hover expectantly near the door.

'Do this in memory of me.' And we look into one another's eyes aware that we are about to suffer a great loss, that our little community is about to be ripped apart, that actions performed speak of betrayal and great suffering. And we are aware that our new sense of community, a community where boundaries have been broken, where hierarchies have the possibility of being reversed, hangs precariously in the balance.

One day the full story will be told, as a tale of struggle and pain, a tale of hope overcoming death, recited by the wisdom of age. The outcome, though, still hangs in the balance, violence and depravity on one side, the possibility of a community and wholeness on the other. For we live in a world of both the cross and the empty tomb, a world where crucifixion and resurrection exist side by side, where we look for hope in relationship with each other, where we look for the Shalom that is holy in the midst of community, where we look for the Divine in the world and in the people around us and we both remember and celebrate in the breaking of bread and the pouring of wine.

This is my body, broken for you. Do this in memory of me.

This is my blood, poured out for you. Do this in memory of me.

For these are the words of the one who embodied love. These are the words of the one who laid down his life for the belief that the world could embody the Shalom of the holy. For these are the words that give us our sense of history, of connectedness with each other and from which we begin to weave relationships of justice and peace within the communities that make up our world.

# Have You Heard the News Today?

*Having two very mature 12-year-olds as part of our church keeps us on our toes and ever mindful of the variety of different media resources we have available for use in worship should we dare! This eucharist derived from a service centring around Pink Floyd's 'The Wall' in which school children are portrayed as mindless robots enslaved by the system. 'All in all you're just another brick in the wall.' Sometimes when faced with the tragedy of news headlines we can feel powerless and enslaved by the system. The video though ends with the school children's rebellion (hence its appeal to teenagers and old alike). We are not just another brick in the wall! So we closed our service by creating our own graffiti wall, rewriting the news headlines to dream of a different reality, a reality where we dare to break conformity to become community.*

Have you heard the news today?

Walls of silence
Walls of fear
Walls to keep you anywhere but near
Walls to keep us isolated
Imprisoned by society's hatred

All in all it's just another brick in the wall
All in all you're just another brick in the wall

Have you heard the news today?

[Rafah lies in ruins...
Insert five headlines from today's international
    news]

All in all it's just another brick in the wall
All in all you're just another brick in the wall

Have you heard the news today?

[Racial violence in...
Insert five headlines from today's national/
    local news]

All in all it's just another brick in the wall
All in all you're just another brick in the wall

Have you heard the news today?

Walls of silence
Walls of fear
Walls to keep you anywhere but near
Walls to keep us isolated
Imprisoned by society's hatred

All in all it's just another brick in the wall
All in all you're just another brick in the wall

Have you heard the news today?
Seen the writing on the wall?
Slogans scrawled across the silence
Graffitied words dispelling fear
Protests breaking walls of isolation

All in all it's not just another brick in the wall
All in all you're not just another brick in the
    wall

Have you heard the news today?
Seen the writing on the wall?
Teacher breaks conformity
Teacher challenges to reconciliation
Teacher invites community

All in all it's not just another brick in the wall
All in all you're not just another brick in the wall

Have you heard the news today?
Seen the writing on the wall?
Grains and grapes of different textures
Host invites to voluptuous banquet
Come and celebrate diversity

All in all it's not just another brick in the wall
All in all you're not just another brick in the wall

Have you heard the news today?
Seen the writing on the wall?
Slogans scrawled across the silence
Graffitied words dispelling fear
Protests breaking walls of isolation

All in all it's not just another brick in the wall
All in all you're not just another brick in the wall

Have you heard the news today?
Seen the writing on the wall?
This is my body broken for you
Do this in confession of all that is divisive
Do this in remembrance of me

Have you heard the news today?
Seen the writing on the wall?
This is my blood poured out for you
Do this in promise of forgiveness
Do this in celebration of me

Let us break the walls of silence
Let us break the walls of fear
Let us break the walls that keep us anywhere but near
Let us dare to break conformity
celebrating diversity woven into community

# Gethsemane

*The dove representing the presence of the Holy Spirit at the baptism of Jesus is a familiar image. We are less familiar with the idea that the Spirit of God was also present in the Garden of Gethsemane.*

On the night when Jesus was betrayed,
On the night when his friends deserted him,
On the night when God's voice was silenced,
On the night all hope was gone,
**The Spirit of God watched,**
**brooding over the face of the deep.**

On the night when they celebrated the festival of Passover,
On the night when they shared a last meal together,
On the night when they spoke of betrayal and death,
On the night when they said their last goodbyes,
**The Spirit of God held her breath...**
**and waited.**

On the night Jesus took bread, ordinary everyday bread,
On the night when in the midst of pain, he gave thanks,
On the night when the master became the servant,
On the night when the tables started to turn,
**The Spirit of God felt anew the swelling within her**
**and the pain of birthing new life.**

On the night when Jesus took wine, meant for partying,
On the night when heaven and hell joined as one,
On the night when wine became a symbol of violence,
On the night before the shroud of religious respectability was ripped apart
**The Spirit of God gently nurtured**
**the fragile stirrings of a new hope.**

And so we too give thanks for the ordinariness of bread

Kneaded bread...     that is the food of the poor,
Pummelled bread...   that is the labour of the exploited,
Broken bread...      that teaches us the difficult lessons of sharing,
Torn bread...        that represents our struggle with the grittiness of life.

...and the extra-ordinariness of wine

| | |
|---|---|
| Rich wine... | that is fragrant and extravagant, |
| Flowing wine... | that is the drink of partying and celebration, |
| Poured wine... | that speaks of loss and remembrance |
| Spilt wine... | that shocks us to the violence of our world. |

And we give thanks for the hope bread and wine offer

| | |
|---|---|
| Hope... | of turning the tables of poverty and injustice, |
| Hope... | of breathing new life into our broken communities, |
| Hope... | of bringing wholeness and integrity to shattered lives, |
| Hope... | of children growing up surrounded by love and stability. |

The Spirit who gives us life also challenges us
to share our lives and our hopes,
to share bread and wine.

This is the ordinary bread
through which Jesus identified
with the pain of human life.
This is for us the bread of heaven
and hope of a more just world.

This is the extraordinary wine
through which Jesus challenges us
to share the pain of human life.
This is for us the wine of new life
and the hope of the Easter dawn.

**The Spirit has watched and waited**
**The Spirit has laboured and given birth**
**The Spirit now invites us to celebrate**
**and to live out our hope of new life.**

# The Voice of Wisdom Calls...

*In Proverbs, the voice of Wisdom is portrayed as wandering the city streets, calling from the unexpected places, calling to those who will listen.*

The voice of Wisdom calls...
to a young child in the darkness of the night, 'Samuel.'
The voice of Wisdom calls...
to an elderly priest whose sight was failing, 'Eli.'
And still the voice of Wisdom beckons us today,
enticing us to seek her.

The voice of Wisdom calls...
to a group of fishermen mending their nets, 'Simon,' 'Andrew'
The voice of Wisdom calls...
to two men talking under a fig tree, 'Philip,' 'Nathanael.'
And still the voice of Wisdom beckons us today,
enticing us to seek her.

The voice of Wisdom calls...
to a woman refusing to give up her seat, 'Rosa Parks.'
The voice of Wisdom calls...
to a Baptist pastor who knew the cost, 'Martin Luther King.'
And still the voice of Wisdom beckons us today,
enticing us to seek her.

The voice of Wisdom calls...
calls from the least expected places,
in the obscenities uttered by children on our crime ridden streets,
in the memories of the frightened and frail,
in the tears of those forced from their homes by hunger or violence,
in the stubborn witness of a tiny, forgotten church.

The voice of Wisdom beckons us today,
calling us by name,
The voice of Wisdom beckons us today,
enticing us to speak her name.

# Consciousness

*We take our worship extremely seriously despite the chaos. What we do matters. We meet in the presence of the living God. It is good, therefore, to stop; to take stock; to be aware of what it is that we think we are doing and who we think we are doing it with.*

Forgiving God,
We gather together
conscious of the times
we've failed ourselves and you.

We gather together
conscious of the times
you've forgiven us and we've forgiven others.

We gather together
conscious of the times
and the need for forgiveness in our world.

# We Cannot Pray

We cannot pray
for the poor
if we walk by on the other side.

We cannot pray
for the hungry
and continue to waste our food.

We cannot pray
for the exploited
and buy the products that enslave them.

We cannot pray
for the persecuted
if we support the bully.

We cannot pray
for the unemployed
and still value only the lowest price.

God of forgiveness,
in this world of sin,
we dare not pray,
for we, ourselves, are ensnared in sin.
Forgive us,
that we cannot live lives without sin
that we cannot escape the systems of death
that we cannot change the world.
Forgive us.
Hear our prayers
and change us
to become part of the solution.

Breaking and Lifting
This Is My Body

Dodging the broken glass on our doorstep has become an everyday reality since we moved next door to an off-licence! The pavements are covered and no one seems to care sufficiently to get it swept up.

Clare used to work in a women's refuge. There, broken glass was a more sinister reminder of damaged and broken community. This is my body, broken for you.

Even in broken bread – or smashed glass – there is a memory of wholeness, a reminder that this is not how things are supposed to be.

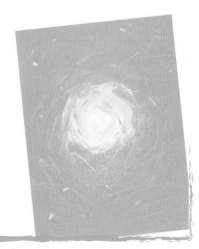

# The Body of Christ Broken:
# The Bread of Lament

## In the Depth of Silence

In the depth of silence
no words are needed,
no language required.
In the depth of silence
I am called to listen...

Listen to the beating of your heart.
Listen to the blowing of the wind,
the movement of the Spirit.
Be silent – said the Lord
and know that I am God.

And listen to the cry of the voiceless.
Listen to the groaning of the hungry.
Listen to the pain of the landless.
Listen to the sigh of the oppressed
and to the laughter of children.

For that is authentic communication;
listening to people
living with people
dying for people.

# Christingle Litany

Voice 1:  We wait in the darkness of long winter nights,
in the darkness we remember our suffering planet;
the earth parched and dry, or flooded and washed away,
the seas polluted, despoiled and robbed of their treasures,
the air heavy, choking with the wastes of modern living.

Voice 2:  We long for the coming of your light,
in the brilliance of light we give thanks for the beauty of the planet;
the earth fertile, springing the seeds of life,
the crystal waters playing over jagged waterfalls,
the skies twinkling with the pinpricks of distant galaxies.

All:  **We light these Christingles as a sign of your joy,
Come Holy Child, lead us from darkness
into the radiance of your dawn.**

Voice 1:  We wait in the darkness of the icy grip of winter,
in the coldness of winter we remember those who have no home;
refugees forced to flee their homelands and their homes,
the homeless who wander our city streets, sleeping rough,
and those whose homes are not places of security, but places of violence and abuse.

Voice 2:  We long for the coming of your warmth,
in the safety and comfort of warmth we give thanks for those around us;
for the welcome and warmth of the places we call home,
for the gathering of families and friends to share and celebrate,
and for those who give of their time and care, working to give others a happy Christmas.

All:  **We light these Christingles as a sign of your love,
Come Holy Child, lead us from darkness
into the radiance of your dawn.**

Voice 1:  We wait in the darkness and dullness of despair,
in the darkness of despair we remember those who live in fear;
victims of the atrocities and horrors of war,
those who live behind closed doors, fearful of walking the city streets,
and those whose lives are ruled by addiction and the need to feed a habit.

Voice 2:  We long for the coming of your light,
in the light of possibilities we give you thanks;
for the hope of peace between our nations,
for fragile relationships, taking cautious steps towards reconciliation,
for the ending of injustice and oppression and the coming of your Shalom.

All:  **We light these Christingles as a sign of your hope,
Come Holy Child, lead us from darkness
into the radiance of your dawn.**

# Wine Confession

*Our house is next door to an off-licence and next door but one to a pub. On a daily basis we see alcohol abused and lives destroyed. Yet wine is one of God's good gifts and the seal on Christ's promise.*

I drink to forget
  forget the emptiness of a life lived only
    for pleasure
  forget the guilt of my selfishness
  forget the unbearable weight of the past

I drink to let go
  let go the constraints of decency
  let go the violence which is hidden inside
  let go the limits on my deepest desires

I drink to dull the pain
  the pain of remembering
  the pain of my loneliness
  the pain of my longing to be loved

God whose promise is sealed in a cup of wine
Forgive us that we take the cup of unity
and use it to divide and abuse
your body
Forgive us our selfish greed
and unite us
into your resurrection community
joining your heavenly hosts
in drinking a toast
to love

Now and for ever

# ASBO Prayer

*Manchester is the ASBO (Anti-Social Behaviour Order) capital of Britain. Crime issues were the highest priority on residents' lists when we began the regeneration project, so some of the first projects we developed were things like CCTV and Neighbourhood Wardens. It would be wrong to say that they have had no effect – crime has fallen – but what has really made a difference is changing people's lives and re-building community.*

Holy God,
So often we want your law to be simple,
a set of rules to follow,
preferably not too demanding,
an easy distinction between what's right
    and wrong.

So often we want your law to be easy,
'forgive and forget' we glibly say,
to absolve us from the need to confront
    our pain,
or to meet the eyes of the one we've hurt.

So often we want your law to be on our terms,
to gather people on our side,
to know that we are in the right
and others are in the wrong.

So often we want the law to make us feel safe,
to exclude those who are different from
    ourselves,
keep out the people our society rejects
and to set ourselves apart in a 'holier than
    thou' huddle.

Holy God,
Your law is not that simple,
not so much rules as a rule of life,
an invitation to understanding,
as people's lives tell a more complex story.

Your law is not that easy
it is an ongoing journey that requires courage,
gently to confront ourselves and others,
measuring our actions against the rule of
    your love.

Your law is not on our terms
or even on the terms of humanity
for love cannot be measured
or forgiveness legislated.

Your law is not there to hide us from the
    dangers of life
but to challenge us to welcome our
    differences,
to include those society seeks to reject,
embodying love in reconciling the conflicts of
    our world.

# Re-membering Women

*This litany was written around Halloween, an ancient festival adopted and adapted by our society into a bizarre costumed excuse to celebrate the macabre. Here we re-member those women, often healers and midwives, persecuted for what was misunderstood as witchcraft, as well as women abused today.*

We gather in an act of remembrance as we
remember our sisters whose cycles of life have
been cut short or prevented from flourishing.

We remember the faceless and often
   nameless women
who were, and are, silenced, raped and
   abused in our religious texts.

We banish the evil of oppression, saying:
**No never again!**

We remember the countless numbers of
   midwives and healers
burned by a state which feared women's
   power to birth and heal.

We banish the evil of oppression, saying:
**No never again!**

We remember the numerous infants and
   young girls
foot-bound and crippled by male designed
   fashion and fetishes.

We banish the evil of oppression, saying:
**No never again!**

We remember the knowing, older women,
   cast out or widowed
drowned by communities who feared their
   independence and wisdom.

We banish the evil of oppression, saying:
**No never again!**

We remember the women forced into
   marriages or prostitution
who simply disappear or are kept in domestic
   and sexual slavery.

We banish the evil of oppression, saying:
**No never again!**

We remember the courageous women who
   claimed and expressed their sexuality
executed by the church for daring to celebrate
   their flesh.

We banish the evil of oppression, saying:
**No never again!**

We remember the determined women who
   campaigned for the right to vote
imprisoned and ridiculed for refusing to be
   silenced.

We banish the evil of oppression, saying:
**No never again!**

[space for remembering and banishing other
forms of oppression of women ending with the
words and response]

We banish the evil of oppression, saying:
**No never again!**

# Thirty Pieces of Silver

*I once had to appear as a witness in a court case. A friend was accused of stealing a large amount of money from an organization we ran together. After several days of evidence, the case was dismissed, leaving all concerned with a bitter taste of injustice.*

Come and join me
You who are rich
and you who are poor
You who are black
and you who are white
You who are young
and you who are old.

Come to this table
Not to show how good you are
but rather because you need to be loved
embraced
accepted.

Wait at the table
Not for the great judge to dispense his
   wisdom
and justice
but wait for your lover
to share his best with you.

Come
Share
Love

For on the night when fairness died, when a friend sold his love for thirty pieces of silver, when Jesus would cry out in vain for justice, that same night, Jesus sat at table with his friends and his betrayer.

He took a piece of bread. When kings were feasting on the best that earth provides, the king of love ate the bread of the poor. He gave thanks to the God who was to abandon him, broke the bread and gave it to them:

This is my body. Broken for you, whoever you are. Eat it. Remember my death. Remember my rage.

In the same way, when they had eaten, he took a cup of wine, the wine of celebration, the wine of abuse. He gave it to them, saying:

This is my blood. Innocent blood shed to unite victim with perpetrator. Blood of covenant. Blood of promise. Blood of hope.

So, we give thanks to God, as Jesus gave thanks all those years ago.

We give thanks to God, even though we sometimes feel the pain of abandonment. And daily see the unfairness of the world God created.

On the news, in our lives, we have seen the depths of that abandonment. As children suffer, and the poor starve, as civilians die and soldiers fight in wars they don't understand, as the planet chokes in the stench of rich businessmen's profits, we give thanks.

We give thanks

We give thanks to God
Whose existence we sometimes question

We give thanks to God
We give thanks to God

Who weeps with us

Who screams with us

Who dies with us

This is my body
This is my blood

This is my future
This is my hope

This is my passion

Do this in remembrance of me

We have stamped our feet, and petulantly
    cried, 'It's not fair!'
We have laid all our anger at the injustice of
    the world
at the foot of your cross
and you have gladly picked it up
In return for our bitterness
you give us bread
In return for our anger
you give us wine
So send down your Spirit upon us
transform our bitterness and anger
into your rage and passion
and send us out into your world
to transform what is not yet
into what can be
Today and tomorrow
Now and for ever
Amen.

# Resurrection Rhythms

*After many years of avoiding our denominational gathering we were persuaded, reluctantly, to attend. The theme of Resurrection Rhythms inspired this eucharist and continues to set our toes tapping as we write this.*

Jesus said to them, 'Come away to a deserted place all by
    yourselves and rest awhile.' For many were coming and
    going, and they had no leisure even to eat.
Come to me all who are weary and I will give you rest,
Come to me, you who seek peace and find only noise,
Come to me, all who would dance to my resurrection rhythm,
Come to me
And join the dance.

For, on the night when the noise finally drowned out
    God's heartbeat,
Jesus gathered his sheep together
in an upper room.
He washed the feet that were learning to dance.
The piper washed their feet.
And as the shouting and screaming grew louder, he dipped
    his bread with the one who screamed loudest. One of you
    will betray me.
One of you will silence my heartbeat.
As the shouting and screaming grew louder, his betrayer
    could take no more and ran away, searching for silence,
    searching for calm.
As the shouting and screaming grew louder, his betrayer
    found only the silence of a suicide tree.
As the shouting and screaming grew louder,
the noise drowned out the silence
the noise drowned out the peace.
A drawn sword,
a cut-off ear
an army of occupation
collaborating elite
hypocritical priests shouting dogmatic certainties
drowning out silence
drowning out peace

Friends together
meet to dance.
A piece of bread
broken
shared.
'Come away to a deserted place all by
    yourselves and rest a while.'
A human body
broken
shared.
'Come away to a deserted place all by
    yourselves and rest a while.'

Friends together
meet to dance.
A cup of wine
poured
shared.
I will gather the remnant of my flock out of all
    the lands where I have driven them, and I
    will bring them back to their fold, and they
    shall be fruitful and multiply.
Pumped blood
poured
shared.
I will gather the remnant of my flock out of all
    the lands where I have driven them, and I
    will bring them back to their fold, and they
    shall be fruitful and multiply.

Be still
Receive my spirit
Be still
Be calm
Receive my peace
Receive my peace
Receive my peace.

This is my body broken for you
This is my heartbeat
This is my blood poured out for you
This is my heartbeat.

You have fed us with your body
refreshed us with your blood.
You have silenced the noise of our troubles
with the heartbeat of your love.
Send us out dancing
Send us out with joy
To live
To love
To listen
To dance the world into life
and be still.

# Blessings and Curses

*Often we are quick to focus on the blessings element of the Sermon on the Mount. Here these are balanced by naming some curses of contemporary life.*

Blessed are you who are poor, for yours is the
    kingdom of God...
and Mary gives birth into the poverty
of a stable
and looks into the eyes of God.

Blessed are you who are hungry, for you will
    be filled...
and a boy's packed lunch is shared out
on a Galilean hillside.

Blessed are you who weep now, for you will
    laugh...
and Sarah whose weeping turned to laughter
gives birth to a son.

Blessed are you when people hate you and
    exclude you...
and Jesus cried in a loud voice
'My God, my God, why have you
    forsaken me?'

Woe to you who are rich, for you have
    received your consolation...
and the rich young footballer
hides in gated isolation.

Woe to you who are full, for you will be
    hungry...
and a college dining room serves only bread
    and water
to remind us how much we take for granted.

Woe to you who are laughing, you will mourn
    and weep...
and one day the consumer-packaged dream
will come crashing down.

Woe to you when people speak well of you,
    for that is what their ancestors did to
    false prophets...
and one day the Church
will cease to be respectable.

For Jesus gathered around ordinary tables
eating with the dis-respectable, the ones with
    no voice...

and we say:
holy, holy, holy, vulnerable God,
the world around us is full of your glory...

Hosanna, let us gather together,
let us take bread and bless it.

Blessed is the one who walks with us in the
    name of God...

Hosanna, let us break bread and share it.

This is my body, broken for you...
This is my blood poured out for you.

We do this in memory of Jesus and in
    celebration of the blessing of life.

# Jesus and Mary

*This strangely long and thin poem/prayer is loosely based on the late – and much lamented – Sydney Carter's song, 'Said Judas to Mary'.*

My body
I leave
with you
My body
torn
bleeding
broken
on the
cross
of the
world

The poor
I leave
with you
The poor
torn
bleeding
broken
on the
cross
of the
world

The poor
are
my body
My body
is
the poor
incarnate
God
in flesh
flesh in
God

Bread
ripped
fragments
dropped
trampled
into
the dust
This is
my body
broken
for you

Wine
splashed
spilt
stained
red
with
violence
This is
my blood
poured out
for you

It is
the poor
we
remember
It is
the poor
from
whom
we seek
forgiveness
It is
the poor
we
embody
It is
the poor
we
celebrate
It is
the poor
who
are
love

The poor have died
The poor have risen
The poor will come again

# Good Samaritan

Who is my neighbour?

There was once a man travelling from Jerusalem to Jericho...
    We pray for all those who are victims of another's violence and greed
    for the nervous woman arriving at the refuge
    for the hungry children walking long distances to the feeding camps in Darfur
    for the isolated man kept in a cage at Guantánamo Bay

when robbers stripped him and beat him and left him for dead...
    We pray for all those who by their actions hurt others
    for the bored youths seeking excitement in the city park
    for the shopping addict who shoplifts from the local store
    for the drunk driver who crashes his car onto the pavement

a priest saw him and walked by on the other side...
    We pray for all those whose piety blinds them to reality
    for the local minister too caught up in meetings to offer a listening ear
    for the public school boy who's never seen a city slum
    for the tourist who fails to question the poverty of a rural beauty spot

a lawyer saw him and walked by on the other side...
    We pray for all those who fail to use their gifts for the purposes of justice
    for the politician who tows the party line rather than asking questions
    for the solicitor who touts for claims work rather than take on difficult cases
    for the teacher who fails to teach children to dream of a better future

an asylum seeker saw him, bandaged his wounds and took care of him...
    We pray for all those who come as outsiders to our community
    for the refugee who is desperate to use skills to contribute to society
    for the anti-social family constantly moved from place to place
    for the child with autism who struggles to relate to others in his class

Who is my neighbour?
    We pray for ourselves that we might become good neighbours
    walking the extra mile and not counting the cost
    caring for others, making them feel included in our community
    challenging poverty and injustice wherever it is found.

# Make Yourself Known

*We see the news on TV and in our newspapers. We do not see God. This simple prayer will need to be updated to reflect the situations where God is not evident today.*

Unseen God
We pray for all those situations where you cannot be recognized:

For *Fallujah*...

For those excluded from our society because of their colour, religion or status...

For *Israel-Palestine*...

For children who leave school with no hope...

For *Openshaw*...

For those whose pain is endless...

Unseen God
You are made known in gentle touch
Make yourself known
and touch your world
in the places we have mentioned
and the people we have named in our hearts
Make yourself known
through us
and use us to touch your world
here
now
and for evermore

# I Only Let Go

*This eucharist is written in the voice of a young child lost in a new country. We have many new refugees and asylum seekers moving into our community. How often do we stop and try to put ourselves into their shoes?*

I only let go for a moment
So many legs
knees
bags
a buggy here
a trolley there
Mum's hand
warm
strong
leading
guiding
gripping
holding

I only let go for a moment

They were so shiny
so exciting
so inviting

I only let go for a moment

and now she is gone
now I am lost

So many legs
knees
bags

I cannot see the warm
familiar
I cannot see my way home

Where am I?
Where do I go?
Where do I belong?

Where do I come from?
Where am I going?
Where is my warm bedroom?
Where are my toys?

I want to go home

I want to go home

I want to go home

This
is not my home
This
is a foreign land
where I do not belong
I cannot play in your fields
I cannot dance in your mud
I cannot hide in your forest

I want to go home

I want to touch familiar grass between my
    toes
I want to feel familiar breezes caress my hair
I want to wipe familiar rain from my eyes

I want to go home

I want the loving comfort of friends
and family
I want to be hugged
I want to be loved

I want to be loved
not tolerated

I want to be loved

*A cross is planted*
*upon a hillside*
*A cross waits*
*silhouetted*
*dark*
*stark*
*against the sky*

Where shall I go?
I do not belong here
This bright shiny world
scares me
I have lost my way
I have lost my path
Where shall I go?

*A cross is rooted*
*in the cool dark earth*
*A cross is planted*
*in the fields of your pain*

This bread comes from the land
This wine comes from the land
This bread comes from God
This wine comes from God

*We offer to God*
*What is God's*

This is my body
broken to root you
in my death

*Drink this all of you*
*Remember the home you have lost*
*and look forward to the land I shall give you*

As we are lost
*Christ has died*

As we are found
*Christ has risen*

As we look forward to the promised land
*Christ will come again*

Send us out
*Send us home*

to live
*to work*

to build a place of shelter and security
*for all your children*
for ever

# We Are Not Alone

*There may only be a small number of us present when we celebrate eucharist and we may use many differing liturgies depending on the theme and context of our worship, but when we gather, we are conscious that as we gather together at Christ's table all of God's people are with us.*

Voice 1:   We meet around this table as friends, as family.
Voice 2:   We meet to share richly, of your goodness, of one another
Voice 3:   We meet to remember
Voice 4:   We meet to forget
Voice 5:   We meet to celebrate all that we have and all that we are.
**All         We meet in the presence of the one who leads us to new life.**

Voice 1:   We meet
Voice 2:   We greet
Voice 3:   We eat
Voice 4:   We drink
Voice 5:   We think
**All         We celebrate**

Voice 1:   We are not alone as we gather
Voice 2:   The refugees are present, who have no home

Voice 3:   We are not alone as we share
Voice 4:   The women are here, excluded from power

Voice 1:   We are not alone as we eat
Voice 2:   The poor are here, who have no bread

Voice 3:   We are not alone as we drink
Voice 4:   The victims are here, bruised by abuse and violence

Voice 1:   We are not alone as we celebrate
Voice 2:   Those whose faith has died are here

Voice 3:   We are not alone as we live
Voice 4:   For the dead are with us too

Voice 5:   In Christ, all humanity is present on earth
             In Christ, all humanity is present here

Voice 1:   In broken bread, we see broken life
Voice 2:   In spilled wine, we see empty rejoicing

Voice 5:   In death we see life

Voice 3:   In bread shared, we see hope
Voice 4:   In wine offered, we see promise

Voice 5:   In death we see life

Voice 1:   Take this bread, broken to remember the body broken, and share it. Take of its goodness, and give generously out of its bounty.

Voice 2:   Take this wine, poured out like blood, and enjoy it. Drink with pleasure, and share hope with those around you.

All:       **We have feasted, let us feast**
**We have received, let us give**
**Let us remember that you go with us**
**And let us go out in the presence of all your people**
**And rejoice.**

# The Body of Christ Re-membered: The Promise of Healing

## Without Condition

*Too often we put boundaries around the love of God. You may only take communion if...*
*Here we celebrate the unconditional love of God.*

This table is where we meet the invisible,
    unknowable God.
This table is where we meet one another.
This table is where we see,
in broken bread
and spilled wine,
the broken body and shed blood
of God's love.
So we invite all to join us in this feast.
Without condition.
If you have loved God for many years,
If you are unsure whether you have ever met God,
If you are drawn to the living God,
join us now.

For we believe that Jesus shared the Passover
    Meal with all who loved him.
In an upper room
among his friends
Jesus took a piece of bread,
unrisen bread,
ordinary, plain human bread,
and as was the custom,
he gave thanks to the God beyond knowing,
made known in Passover Bread,
then broke the bread
and gave it to them
'This is my body, broken for you.'

In the same way, after supper,
he took a cup of wine,
wine of rejoicing,
wine of celebration
'This is my blood, poured out in eternal promise,
lo, I am with you always.'

So, as Jesus gave thanks,
we give thanks to the God who floats, just
    beyond our grasping,
whose love and creative power, we experience
today and every day,
whose being
we sense
but can never pin down.

We give thanks to the creator
who gave and gives
Life.
We give thanks to all
who have made God known to us.
We give thanks
to Jesus of Nazareth
who lived with us,
died with us,
and whose resurrection leads us into the hope
that there can be, must be
More.

110

We give thanks to the Spirit
who dances in our hearts,
recognizing God
in those we meet,
in those we love,
challenging,
inspiring,
celebrating,
creating,
birthing possibility,
birthing possibility,
in us,
and through us,
now and for ever.

## In This Special Place

*Our much-loved church building is reaching the end of its life. It's shabby and coming a bit loose at the seams but it is the place where we meet God.*

In this special place
At this special time
**We come to meet God.**

In this ordinary place
At this ordinary time
**God is here.**

In all places
At all times
**We join God's people
And worship.**

Mysterious God,
you have given us a glimpse of yourself,
not in gold and jewels,
not in splendour and majesty,
but here,
in bread and wine,
in friends and friendship.
So send us out
in the name of the world-changing baby,
and the strength of the laughing Spirit,
to make known your crucified,
     world changing
Love,
today
and every day.

## Look Around You

Look around you,
the earth is gripped by the frosts of winter,
autumn leaves – red, gold and brown,
trampled, turn to mush under our feet,
fertilizing the soil
ready for the springing of new life.

Look around you,
the table is prepared for the supper,
the aroma of rich, velvety wine
poured out in memory
of a life given in love for us
sign of hope and new life in Christ.

Look around you,
we are members of one community
just as many grains of wheat
are worked and kneaded into dough,
so we too are gathered at this table
to witness to the peace of Christ.

111

# Memories Shared

*Amidst the bustle of credit union, complementary therapies and gentle exercise class, drop-in regulars put the world to rights around the coffee table. Community is built over a few old black and white photographs or a newly published local history book.*

Memories shared,
stories told,
friendships formed,
spinning the dreams of old.

Questions asked,
power challenged,
outcasts touched,
traditions and lives turned round.

Bread broken,
wine poured,
friends gathered,
in thanksgiving a meal is enjoyed.

Memories shared,
stories told,
friendships formed,
spinning the dreams of old.

Friends deserting,
soldiers arresting,
a man dying,
as hopes lie buried in the ground.

Dawn breaking,
a man awaking,
women greeting,
reunited friends celebrating.

Memories shared,
stories told,
friendships formed,
spinning the dreams of tomorrow.

Gathering together,
the table spread,
confession made,
thanksgivings said.

Bread broken,
wine poured,
take eat, drink,
remember the dream.

Memories shared,
stories told,
friendships formed,
spinning the dreams of tomorrow.

The body of Christ.
The wine of new life.

God of yesterday,
God of today,
God of the days still to come,
you spin the memories of our lives...
you spin the stories that make our lives...
you spin the dreams that give meaning
        to our lives...
Teach us to treasure the memories we have,
Help us to share our stories with one another,
And inspire us to spin our dreams into
        our future.

# The Cross

*This eucharist explores the idea of the cross as a mirror in which we see ourselves and our world. It is in gathering at Christ's table that the broken fragments come together and we see ourselves as the whole, celebrating community Christ intended.*

Sharp, jagged, splintered, glinting,
Our world lies broken,
In fragments as broken glass,
broken by violence,
broken by hate,
broken by greed,
broken by fear.

Sharp, jagged, splintered, glinting,
We lie broken,
In fragments as broken glass,
broken by pain,
broken by anger,
broken by loss,
broken by despair.

On the night he was betrayed,
Jesus took bread,
Bread made from many grains,
mirroring his life,
mirroring our own lives,
and he broke it, saying,
'Do this in memory of me.'

On the night he was betrayed,
Jesus took wine,
Wine made from many grapes,
mirroring his life,
mirroring our own lives,
and he poured it, saying,
'Do this in memory of me.'

And so in this sacrament,
In this breaking of bread and pouring of wine,
Jesus gave thanks,
thanks mirrored in his own love of life,
thanks mirrored in his own ability to touch,
thanks mirrored in his own appreciation
    of beauty,
thanks mirrored in his own celebration of hope.

And so in this sacrament,
In this breaking of bread and pouring of wine,
We give thanks,
thanks mirrored by our love of justice,
thanks mirrored in our concern for others,
thanks mirrored in our work for peace,
thanks mirrored in our celebration of life.

The bread of life is broken for the life
    of the world.

The wine of heaven is poured for the
    healing of the world.

And so through this sacrament,
In this breaking of bread and pouring of wine,
The broken fragments come together,
mirroring the strength that leads to healing,
mirroring the courage that speaks of hope,
mirroring the relationships that recreate
    community,
mirroring the love that will not let us go.

# Easter

Today is the day of promise
Today is the day when our hopes
 find their focus
Today is the day when your cross
 stands empty
And we see the stone rolled from your tomb

Today is the day
When women lead the way
Simply believing
Simply hoping

Today is the day
When all creation groans in anticipation
Of the resurrection
Which your resurrection promises

So come
Eat, drink and make merry
For Christ is risen from the dead

Christ is risen from the dead

And we shall rise with him!
And we shall rise with him!
And we shall rise with him!

At Easter, in Easter
We see the agony of Good Friday
When God died
When God was left hanging on a
 cross of wood

At Easter, in Easter
We see the humiliation of the most lovely
Despised and rejected
Scourged and crucified
As your children suffer still

Yet in that cruellest of agonies
We find our hope and our joy
In crumpled cloths and a rolled away stone
We see the buds of new life
And claim your promise

So in meeting here
To take bread and wine
We touch holy ground
With fear and trembling
We break the bread of life
And take the cup of promise
From hands pierced with nails
Pierced with love

In bread and wine
We look back
To your death and resurrection

In bread and wine
We look forward
In eager anticipation
Of the time when all things shall be
 born again

For on the night when even love and
 friendship failed
Jesus took a piece of bread
He gave thanks
Facing death, Jesus gave thanks
And offered the bread to the friends who
 had failed him
And who would fail him

Take and eat. This is my body
I give it freely to you
Remember me when you break bread

Then after supper
He lifted a cup of wine
Again he gave thanks
In the midst of his sorrow, he gave thanks
And passed it around the company
And on to us

Drink this, all of you
For in this wine is my promise to you
And to all the world sealed in my blood

Christ's promise is true
Today, at Easter
As at every eucharist
We recall with awe and wonder
In the midst of sorrow and suffering
The love which could not die
The love which cannot die

# Hope Against Hope

*Frequently our Christian hope is a 'hope against hope'. For hope to be real, it must face up to the 'hope-less' reality of the world. This call to worship came out of a particularly depressing time in our life together.*

God of justice
we come from a world
where the most powerful have their way
and violence speaks louder than words

God of justice
we come from a community
where trust has been violated
and our confidence in justice has been shaken

God who restores justice
we come from our broken lives
seeking your wisdom and counsel
hoping for the restoration of your Shalom

# Call to Resurrection

*Living in the heart of an urban regeneration area we have reflected a great deal on the language of regeneration which, in its most visionary moments, echoes the biblical call to resurrection and has kindled our imagination.*

May the God who calls us to resurrection,
    give us the courage to share our stories;

May the God who calls us to recreation,
    share our tears and heal our brokenness;

May the God who calls us to remembrance,
    stand alongside us in our struggle for
    justice and peace;

May the God who calls us to regeneration,
    work with us in making our dreams for this
    community and for this world into reality;

In the name of the one who is love.

# Upsetter of Pious Religion

*Some churches find our ways a little challenging. We looked at Jesus overturning the tables with a neighbouring church and set about up-turning their communion table. This was a step too far and we were politely told to use the nearby coffee table instead.*

Do this in memory of me.

Do this in memory of Jesus
born in the poverty of a stable,
who lived in an occupied land,
oppressed by the strangers' hand.
Carpenter's son
Leper's friend
Lover of tax collectors and sinners
Rebel
Outcast
Upsetter of pious religion.

Whoever, therefore, eats the bread or drinks
the cup of the Lord in an unworthy manner
will be answerable for the body and blood of
the Lord.

We remember the crucified one
hung on a cross by inhumane soldiers
obeying orders
to torture and humiliate.
We remember the victims
of suicide bombers
following a creed
of vengeance and despair.

Examine yourselves, and only then eat of the
bread and drink of the cup.

We remember our riches
and the poverty we forget.
We remember the despair
that our power brings to those
who have no choice.
We remember the brokenness
of a world created in God's image.

For all who eat and drink without discerning
the body, eat and drink judgement against
themselves.

Hear the word of the Lord, all you that enter
the gates to worship. Amend your ways and
your doings, and let me dwell with you in this
place. Do not trust in these deceptive words:
'This is the temple of the Lord, the temple of
the Lord, the temple of the Lord.'

We remember our own part
in unjust systems and structures
which make the rich richer
and starve the poor.
We remember our failure to challenge
the leaders who support violence
and oppression.
We remember our apathy
in the face of the cynicism
of political systems
which murder the innocent
in the search for electoral success.

And so,
with Christ
we take bread
with Christ
we give thanks for all we have received
with Christ

we break the bread
with Christ
we share the bread
with Christ
we see his broken body.

This is my body that is for you. Do this in
remembrance of me.

With Christ
we take the cup
With Christ
we share the promise
With Christ
we promise eternal love to all
With Christ
we remember all the victims
and will not let them die

This cup is the new covenant in my blood. Do
this, as often as you drink it, in remembrance
of me.

God,
you have changed us
with your body and blood.
God,
you have challenged us
with your body and blood.
God,
you have empowered us
with your body and blood.
Send us out
into your world
to change
to challenge
and to empower
in Jesus' name.

# Up-turned Table

*At Mersey Street the congregation came in to find the communion table turned over with copper coins strewn across the front of the church and the bread and wine laid on a crumpled cloth on the floor. Their response was to take their seats and remark that we must be looking at the story of the turning over of the tables of the money lenders!*

God of the up-turned tables
God of the poor
God of the outcast
God of the down trodden

God who is not afraid to be angry
God who is not afraid to be vulnerable
God who is not afraid to be weak
God who is not afraid to be foolish

We come to your up-turned table
We come to the scene of chaos
We come to bread ripped apart in violence
We come to wine spilt as blood

We come to your up-turned table
Bringing the brokenness of our world
Bringing a world where wealth and power
Speak louder than justice and peace

We come to your up-turned table
Voicing the longing of our world
A world where beauty flourishes
A world where hope cannot be crushed

On the night before the tables were violently
    turned
And the curtain of religious exclusion was torn
    apart
On the night before the tree of life became a
    cross of death
Jesus took bread and wine

And we give you thanks for the gift of bread
Bread that is the sustenance of life
Bread that speaks of equality and justice
Bread that speaks of the tables starting to
    turn

And we give you thanks for the gift of wine
Wine that speaks of celebration in the midst
    of destruction
Wine that speaks of hope in the midst of
    despair
Wine that speaks of new life in the midst of
    violence and war

Let us share the bread that teaches us of the
    hope we have in community
Let us share the wine that teaches us of
    forgiveness and celebration

God of the up-turned tables
Challenge us to turn the tables on the misuse
    of power
Challenge us to turn the tables on prejudice
    wherever it is found
Challenge us to turn the tables on violence
    and live peace

God of the up-turned tables
Help us to live the foolishness that is gospel
Help us to live out heaven in the midst of hell
Help us to live lives that celebrate hope

# Enemy of Apathy Blessing

*In a church of less than twenty members, unless every member is prepared to get involved, nothing happens! We do not have room for apathy. The Iona song, 'Enemy of Apathy', on which this prayer and the eucharist which follows are based has become a favourite.*

May the blessing of the God
who broods over the waters of chaos
be with us.

May the blessing of the Son
who walks through the waters of baptism
be with us.

And may the blessing of the Spirit
who alights bringing hope
   to our ravaged world
be with us.

Now and evermore.

## Enemy of Apathy

Brooding, birthing, sighing, singing, nurturing, holding, like a bird breathing life into creation, the Spirit gathers us under her wings; calling us into community, the Spirit re-members us, re-creates in us, and entrusts to us — Creating, weaving, transforming, daring, dreaming, eternal love, breathing resurrection into community. Winging, soaring, lighting, resting, nesting, welcoming, rushing wind rippling through the corn, the Spirit quickens 'ging, breaks bread, pours wine, bleeds and dies. — inspiring, meaning, incarnated presence, word made flesh, human and divine, the Spirit gives thanks, breaks bread — Dancing, roaring, startling, waking, fanning the dough, baking bread, the oven's flame.

## The Path to Emmaus

footprints
  in the   travel   the
  sand    on   journey  from
                    birth
    Life, transient         to
    like the impression    death
  of footprints on a beach
  swept away by the rising tide
  the journey smooth in places
  painfully rocky in others
   a journey from birth
   to death. Emmaus
    footprints heavy
    at first then
    scuffed, hurried
    running, dancing
    the road from
    death to life.
  The cross becomes
  resurrection as
  humanity skips
  hand in hand
  with God.

## Rhythmic Chaos

Lord of the dance
dancing on the
  graveyard
of sin and death
  of suspicion and
    division
  of shame
    and dis-
    ease
  Yours is not
   the
   genteel
   dance
  of royal court
  or ballet stage
Your moves are
  not
  choreographed
Your arms wave
  wildly
Your legs fly with
  rhythmic abandon
as your body whirls to the
  music
Your dance
  is passion
   Your dance
    is commitment
    Your dance
    is love
     Your dance
     is life
    unending
   life
  indefinable
life

unquenchable
life
Your dance
goes on
wild
strange
mad
foolish
dancing
foolish
dancing
fool
laughing
fool
loving
fool
dancing in the
  face of death
dancing on the
  face of
  death
dancing
prancing
whirling
spinning
see the dance
feel the dance
feel the rhythm
  feel the joy
  join the dance
   dance
   dance wherever you
   may be
  join the dance
   follow me
   join the dance
   of folly
    join the dance
    of love.

# Dancing Fool

*'Don't know much about dancing,*
*That's why I got this song.*
*One of my legs is shorter than the other*
*'n' both of my feet's too long'*

*I wonder if this is the only eucharistic prayer ever to be based upon a Frank Zappa song? You may be able to spot one or two other musical references.*

The day the music died
The night the song was
    silenced
Stopped
Controlled
Packaged
Sold
The dancing fool
invited his friends
instructed his friends
to keep dancing.
When the music stops
keep dancing.
Dance together
Dance with one another
Dance with the silent one
Dance with the one who
    cannot keep still.
So, on this Easter morning
our toes tapping
our feet itching
our fingers tapping
the rhythm of life
we gather together
to join the dance.

We dance with the one who
    knew silence
We dance with the one who
    knew death

We dance with the one who,
    on the night the music died
shared bread and wine
with those he loved
with those who loved him
and with those who feared him.
He dipped bread with the one
whose view of the world
    needed order
for whom the dance was too
    wild and chaotic.
And still he danced.

He took a piece of bread
Foolishly seeing life
and broke it.
Take, eat, this is my body
broken
silenced
for you.

He took a cup of wine
not the wine of despair
but the wine of folly
and celebration
and shared it with them.
This is my blood.
This is my promise.
This is my music.
Take

Drink
Dance
Remember
Take
Drink
Dance
Remember
Take
Drink
Dance
Remember.

Dancing fool
we gather together
to dance with you.
The music has died
The music has risen
The music will play again.

Dance then
wherever you may be
Dance then
Dance now
Dance for ever!

# Sharing the Cup
## Restoring Relationship

Rachel produced this artwork we've called 'Rachel's World' when she was just ten years old to go on the cover for Clare's ordination service. It represents the dreams of a child, and thus of our congregation, for an inclusive community holding hands around the globe. Celebration of diversity is also the theme of the 'Rainbow Haven', a refugee and asylum seeker drop-in project held locally. In the 'Rainbow Haven' there is a recognition that people's lives have been broken, but here is a chance to make a new life, to begin to restore the broken relationships of our world and make the dream of 'Rachel's World' a reality.

# Embodying the Word

*This opening prayer was co-written with Lis Mullen*

Word of God, human face,
    We arrive at this place, this time,
    our paths merging,
    to join in praise to you.

You spoke your word,
    spoke creation into being,
    spoke love into life,
    spoke chaos into peace.
You said, 'I am for you'.

You became your word,
    earth's fond guest,
    displayed a human face,
    became one with humankind,
You said, 'I am for you'.

You invite us to embody your word,
    speak our lives into love,
    speak our individualism into community,
    speak our complacency into action,
We say, 'We are for you'.

# Dem Bones

*We're getting on a bit. We're tired. The building is crumbling around us. So it's no surprise that the image of dry bones has some resonance!*

I looked at the church
and I saw
a valley of dry bones
Old bones
Tired bones
Dried-up bones
Lonely bones

Come unto me,
all who are heavy laden
all who are dried up
and I will give you rest

For my yoke is easy
My word is life
Love one another, as I have loved you.

And he breathed on them and said,
Receive the Holy Spirit
Peace be with you

Peace be with you
Peace draw you together
Peace unite you
Peace

the peace of God
be always with you.

[share the peace]

And in peace we are united
In peace we are joined
In peace we are community
In peace we are a people
God's people
Christ's people
Christ's body
The body of Christ.

And there was a noise, a rattling and the bones came together. Bone to its bone.

Receive the Holy Spirit
Receive life
Receive Life

For on the night when there was no life
When death triumphed
When unity was destroyed
One man continued to love
One man shared bread with his friends.
Take, eat, this is my body

And there were sinews on them, and flesh had come upon them, and skin had covered them.

After supper, he took a cup of wine
This cup is the new relationship,
sealed by my blood
Life-giving blood,
waking the flesh,
fuelling muscles,
healing wounds.

And the breath came into them, and they
lived, and stood on their feet, a vast multitude.

And all the saints,
on earth
and in heaven
stood up
stand up
in praise
in unity
in love
for one another
and the world.
A people
A body
making God known
building Shalom.

# Re-storation

In a broken world
you join us together
In a land of injustice
you join us together
In the loneliness of the city
you join us together.

Join us together
as your body
in this place
at this moment
Join us together
to celebrate
and worship you.

127

# Stay with Us

*This simple eucharist was woven around three songs from the Iona Community's* Love from Below *and quotes the New Revised Standard Version of Luke 24.28-31. The cup is a cup of promise. Relationship is not yet restored. Our faith is the hope of restored community.*

 [Come, Lord, Be Our Guest]

Voice 1: As they came near the village to which they were going, he walked ahead as if he were going on. But they urged him strongly, saying, 'Stay with us because it is almost evening and the day is now nearly over.' So he went in to stay with them. When he was at the table with them, he took bread, blessed and broke it, and gave it to them. Then their eyes were opened and they recognized him; and he vanished from their sight.

Voice 2: Stay with us,
for the day is far spent
and we have not yet recognized your face in each of our brothers and sisters.

Voice 3: Stay with us,
for the day is far spent
and we have not yet shared your bread
in grace with our sisters and brothers.

Voice 4: Stay with us,
for the day is far spent
and we have not yet listened to your Word
on the lips of our brothers and sisters.

Voice 5: Stay with us,
for the day is far spent
and we have not yet drunk of your wine
or danced in joy with our sisters and brothers.

All: **Stay with us**
**because in the darkness of our night**
**only your presence brings us light.**

 [The Broken Body]

Voice 1:    As we break bread with one another
Voice 2:    Give us your spirit of generosity
Voice 3:    As we enjoy each other's company
Voice 4:    Give us the humility to listen
Voice 5:    And may we drink the wine of celebration, not escape.

All:        **Stay with us**
            **because in the darkness of our night**
            **only your presence brings us light.**

[Bread is blessed]

All:        **Stay with us**
            **because in the darkness of our night**
            **only your presence brings us light.**
            **AMEN**

# The Path Already Trodden

*Much of what we do is new and exciting. However, it is important to us to remember that we belong to a tradition, a history. We are one small part of the story of Shalom.*

We do not wander blindly
into the desert
We are not sent
without a guide.

We are not sheep,
shepherded into the unknown
the untravelled path
the untried pasture
the unsprung trap
for fear of what comes behind us.

We follow the path already trodden
We go where one has gone before
We go where generations have sought to go
We seek to go
We seek to follow
We seek to be disciples
pupils
followers.

We follow the one
who, on the night he was sold
into the unknown by his friends
took a piece of bread
and tore it apart, saying
This is my body, I give it for you.

In the same way, after supper
he took a cup of wine
and shared it with them
This is my blood,
poured out as a promise
that I will always go before you.

And so we give you thanks
you who have trodden the path before us
you who have known the pain and suffering
you who have hoped and feared
you who have shared the anticipation
    of what is not
but what may be.

As we stand
at the foot of the cross
we gaze in awe
at the love which death could not extinguish
and pray for justice
which still eludes our grasp.

 [we pray for justice]

As we face the bloodshed and the violence
with which you met your end
we gaze in awe
at the strength
which did not resort to the violence
of self-defence.

 [we pray for peace]

As we reflect on bread torn apart
on your body broken,
we gaze in awe
at the creative power
which brings all things to be
frustrated by our destructiveness.

 [we pray for the unity of creation]

So now
with eyes open
we take the bread with trembling hands
knowing and not knowing
where such sharing leads.

With joy
we share the bittersweet taste
of your festal wine
and pledge ourselves
to follow.

**Go before us, to light the way**
**Go behind us to comfort and encourage us**
**Go with us**
**Go with us**
**Go with us.**

131

# Weaving Shalom

*Although today we are watching the surviving mills and factories converted into luxury apartments and offices, Manchester was built upon the textile industry. That memory remains part of our communal story.*

Weaving God,
You gather us together
as multicoloured fibres
to weave community.

You gather us together
as textured strands
to celebrate life in all its fullness.

You gather us together
as rainbow threads
to spin your vision of Shalom.

Weaving God,
We gather in community
to celebrate your presence within us
to share our stories and our dreams
and to spin the future together.

# Spinning Yarns

*When I first read this blessing, I immediately imagined God as a gnarled old sailor, with a great white beard and a pipe telling tall tales to an audience of awed young children. Probably the only time we will ever imagine God as a white-bearded old man!*

May the blessing of the God who pulsed
    stories into life;
The blessing of the Child who enacted the
    riding of a donkey into the conflict torn city
    of Jerusalem;
And the blessing of the Spirit who calls us to
    share our stories around a table;
Be with us, as together we learn to speak
    love's name.

# One of Us

*It is all too easy to fall into the trap of projecting our vices or fears onto others. To pray for them 'out there,' rather than to admit that we are part of an imperfect humanity. Here we pray to the one who chose to share in our imperfect humanity.*

Christ our king
born in a stable
adorned with straw
and honoured by cattle,
we bring our petitions to you this morning
knowing that you will hear us.
For you are not enthroned on high,
but rather one of us.

We pray for those who seek power in this
    world...
Show us the way of humility.

We pray for the rich...
Show us the beauty of sharing.

We pray for those who impose their will by
    violence...
Show us the path of peace.

We pray for those who are certain of their
    superiority...
Show us the wisdom of the meek.

We pray for those who twist and distort the
    truth...
Show us the light of your truth.

We pray for those who have given up...
Show us the hope of your eternal life.

Jesus our brother
crucified on a wooden cross
mocked by soldiers
scorned by the religious,
we bring our requests to you this morning
knowing that you will hear us.
For you are not enthroned on high,
but rather lifted up upon a cross
and alive for evermore.

# One Fine Day in the Middle of the Night...

*Traditional theological language usually leaves us cold. Traditional theological language leaves us especially cold when it contradicts itself. Yet somehow the contradiction of a transcendent/ immanent God is one we return to time and again.*

Transcendent God, distant and strange,
God of a nation, but not my nation,
Holy yet unapproachable,
Hidden behind splendour and wealth.

Creating God, present everywhere,
God of all peoples, yet known by none,
Holy yet impassive,
Hidden behind the pomp of religious ceremony.

Self-giving God, born into human poverty,
God for all peoples, known by many,
Holy yet vulnerable,
Hidden behind the mundaneness of daily life.

Immanent God, lived out in community,
God of diversity, known through the richness
     of many traditions,
Holy yet passionate,
Hidden behind the insignificance of many
     people's lives.

Transcendent, Creating, Self-giving,
     Immanent God,
God reflected in the myriad of life that
     teems on Earth,
Imaged in the rich diversity of human experience,
Symbolized simply in bread and juice
     squeezed from fruit.

Jesus shared many meals with his friends
     and strangers,
not from jewel encrusted goblets and
     golden plates,

but from a simple shared earthenware cup
and a broken pottery plate.

At this meal of sharing,
Jesus took ordinary bread, the basis of life,
and charged it with meaning,
This is my body, broken for you.

At this meal of sharing,
Jesus took a simple cup of wine, the luxury
     of celebration,
and charged it with meaning,
This wine is the new relationship with God.

And so as we commune round this table
     we give thanks,
for the stuck-back-together Salvadoran plate,
reminder of peoples across the world
who have much to teach us,
And we remember that the biblical stories
teach us that God is known in many
     different ways.

And we give thanks
for the broken bread, the basis of life,
reminder of the peoples across the world
who lack the resources for basic living,
And we remember that God was
     made known in Jesus
to share the Good News with those society
     had neglected and rejected.

And we give thanks
for the simple, earthenware cup,

reminder to recognize the sacred
among the ordinary down-to-earthness of life.
And we remember that Jesus lived and died
among ordinary people, friends and strangers.

And we give thanks
for the richness of wine,
reminder of the cost of human violence
and the tragedy of human sin.
And we remember those who struggle and die
as a result of humanity's failing to live in
      community.

So come gather round this table with one
      another,
gather round these symbols taken from
      everyday life,
gather round to remember Jesus who lived
      and died
showing us how to live in community with one
      another and with God.

Transcendent, Creating, Self-giving,
      Immanent God,
Holy yet vulnerable,
Holy yet passionate,
known to us through Jesus of Nazareth
and through the people around us,
Send us out from here to live our lives
reflecting your diversity,
reflecting your compassion,
walking with those who suffer,
yet walking towards the hope
of your Shalom.

# Seeing the Unseen

Unseen God
You call us to meet you
In the gurgle of a baby
In the shout of children playing
In the smile of a grandparent.
You call us to meet you
In the kindness offered to a stranger
In the welcome for a refugee
In the coffee for a neighbour.
You call us to meet you
In the comfort of familiar friendship
In the joy of new meeting
In the desire for connection.
You call us to meet you
here
today
with these people
And
here
today
in this group of people
we see your face.

# Seeing God

In your face I see the face of God
In your touch I feel the touch of God
In your eyes I see the love of God
Thank you for sharing God with me

# Power and Glory

*Last week I finally had an opportunity to get my only-worn-once ball gown out from the wardrobe to wear to a black-tie dinner in celebration of five years regeneration. Five years ago, the idea of a formal dinner for the residents of East Manchester would have been viewed as patronizing and divisive. Now, however, the Lord Mayor, MP and councillors mingled joyfully with the many officers and residents who have worked so hard to re-build our community.*

We meet around this table of celebration
to celebrate
not our own successes and achievements
not our own righteousness and glory
but yours.

For you are the God who calls us together
You are the God who invites us to your table
You are the God who tells us to overcome our
    feelings of inadequacy and to pray
to you
the God who invites
the God who forgives
the God who understands.

For you were born
not into the comfort and affluence of western capitalism
but into the victimized squalor of a stable in Bethlehem
Palestine, an occupied, Third World country.

But you did not hate those who victimized you.
You accepted gifts from the Magi
You did not seek revenge upon the rich young ruler
You did not send Nicodemus away.

But nor did you fawn in their presence.
You did not accept their power
You were not ensnared by their wealth.

To all who approached you
you gave the challenge of a new life
a new beginning
a new hope.

You called all who wished to follow you
into a new way of living together
of sharing
of caring
and, by way of demonstrating your sharing
when the ways of this world were
    in the ascendancy
when the clouds of death were gathering
you took a piece of simple bread
broke it, and when you had given thanks
you shared it with your friends.
Take, eat. This bread is really my body
I share it with you
And the next day, you shared even your life
broken
on an oppressor's cross.
But before that, after supper
you took a cup of wine
and shared it with your friends.
This shared cup is my blood
poured out for you
a new way of living
a new relationship of sharing
Drink this, all of you.
Remember me, and hope for my Shalom.

God our hope
you have shown us a new way of life
You have offered us a vision
and invited us to live that dream
So, as we leave this place
travel with us
and show us the way.

# no borders

*One of the churches in our ecumenical group lies on the border with Droylsden. Their priorities are different; their mission is different; their way of being church is different. This is a church with a memory of 'how church should be'. They even sing the Lord's Prayer! Yet we share communion. There are no borders.*

God
Three-in-One
You have drawn us together
in this place
at this time
Different faces
different reasons for coming together
Drawn together by the one God
who models for us
the unity of diversity.
Creator
by whose word we have our life
Redeemer
who loves us in spite of our unloveliness
Sustainer
the energizing Spirit of unquenchable love.
One God
Three faces.

In you, there are no borders
You created one world.
In you, there are no borders
You knew the life of a homeless refugee.
In you, there are no borders
Your restless Spirit blows where she wills.

Forgive us, then
the walls we build to divide country from
    country.
Forgive us, then
the walls we build to hide from one another.
Forgive us, then
the walls which divide faith from faith
and people from you.

Draw us together
and make us friends
with each other
and with you.

Draw us together
and use us to make friends
with each other
with you
and with those with whom we disagree.

Draw us together
and in our unity
teach us to sing with your harmonies, as we
    join together in the great Christian prayer:

Our Father...

# The Rocks Beneath Our Feet

*The City of Manchester Stadium, where the 2002 Commonwealth Games took place, dominates our skyline. Beneath the surface, though, lies a hidden past: the old Bradford Colliery and Gas Works. Residents have even complained that our beloved B of the Bang sculpture does nothing to commemorate the lives that were spilled onto the rocks in the miles of tunnels underground.*

The rocks beneath our feet
fossilize a past world that teamed with life;
The coal beneath our feet
harbours the energy of organic matter;
The water beneath our feet
is bursting with microscopic life;
The trees and plants around us
breathe the air that gives us life.

God of life
your breath is in the earth beneath our feet
your breath is in the water which gives us life
your breath is in the air which we all breathe.
Breathe through us as we gather together
to celebrate the one who gives us life.

# Heartbeat of the Earth

*I like to think that the earth has a memory. Dust to dust, ashes to ashes, earth is made up of the bones of our ancestors. There is a sense that the earth remembers, that the earth itself is scarred by the storms of human life. Maybe this is why so many spiritual traditions draw inspiration from the earth and from nature.*
*This poem draws on the well-known phrase from Julian of Norwich, a fourteenth-century mystic: all is well and all shall be well.*

I stood in the depth of the forest
when dawn pauses to draw breath,
this place, where broken dreams
are held and nurtured,
is sacred, holy ground.

Holy ground,
ground of our being,
being in the midst of life's storms
as they rage, and rip
and tear the fragility of life apart.

Here where the scars run deep
and dying leaves caress the ground,
Here where stones hold on to memories
and ancient trees whisper their testimonies,
Here where the dew drops kiss the
    well-spring of life
and transcendence rises in the ancient
    yearnings of the earth,
Here the song dancer takes the faltering
    first steps
all is well and all shall be well.

# Beauty Poured Out

*The story of the woman at Bethany has to be my all time favourite. Maybe it is because here we have a woman ministering to Jesus. A sensuous, erotic woman whose extravagant, if somewhat unusual, gift of touching another's pain is honoured and celebrated. If we are to become community restored we first have to be prepared to touch each other's pain.*

Extravagant God
We praise you
for the rich
diversity of life
for the many colours
and fragrances
textures
and flavours
that we see
smell
touch
taste
and enjoy.

And we think
of the woman
at Bethany
who was not afraid
to show her love
and concern
not afraid
to touch
another's
pain
and be accepted
in return.

Help us
to appreciate
the beauty of life
and to share
our sense of wonder
with others
Help us to
feel loved
to love ourselves
and to share
your love
with those around us.

# Learning to Speak
## Love's Name

*Stories are central to our life together. Stories remind us of our past, the people who've gone before us. Stories express our identity in the present. Stories dream our future into being. Here is our re-working of the big story, as together, around the table, we learn to speak love's name. You may also notice that it is a re-working of The Silent God (p.70). Words, stories out of silence.*

In the beginning
before God spoke
before the breath of God swept across the waters
in the beginning of the story
there was silence.

Listen to the sound of God
listen to the silence
listen to the pulse of life
out of which God speaks
out of which God calls.

In the beginning
God spoke
and creation exploded into its myriad of forms
at the beginning of the story
life yearned for diversity.

Come to me
come and hear again
my word
my story
my name.

As creation unfolded
God listened
as people created their own stories and traditions

as the story of creation unfolded
people began to speak their own
        names for God.

Come to each other
come and share again
your words
your stories
your names.

As humanity grew older
God wept
as people began to argue over stories
        and territories
as the story of humanity grew older
violence was committed in God's name.

Listen to the sound of God
listen to the cries of a baby
listen to the silence of a cross
out of which God speaks
out of which God calls.

Come ...
come from your palaces and shacks
Gather ...
gather from your cathedrals and brothels
Share ...
share your different cultures and faiths.

Hear again the story which brings us to
        this table:
on the night when all stories came to an end,
Jesus sat at table with friends and betrayers,
to share in the Passover story,
to share in his people's story.

He took a piece of traditional bread,
unleavened bread, made in the rush of escape,
gave thanks to God
and broke it.

He gave it to them, saying:
Take, eat, remember,
and in years to come,
re-tell, this story,
whenever you break bread together.

After supper he took a flask of wine,
wine over which many stories are told,
gave thanks to God
and poured it.

He shared it with them, saying:
This is the covenant of forgiveness,
sealed with my promise,
sealed with my blood.
Drink it and re-member.

And so we share bread,
made in creation,
broken in remembrance.

And so we share wine,
made in heaven,
spilled in forgetfulness.

And so we share our lives and our stories
our different cultures and traditions
our diverse lands and lifestyles
our numerous dreams and aspirations
our shared love and our promises
and as we speak love's name
send us out
to tell your story,
to live your word
to celebrate your many names
from now into eternity.

# Beaufort Spirit

*The biblical image of the Spirit – or breath of God – has often been tamed. At Pentecost the Spirit came as a rushing wind. Powerful and frightening. Living on a long, straight road, we know something of the destructive power of the easterly wind. Others have experienced far greater extremes of the weather measured on the Beaufort Scale. Shalom, peace, must embrace the whole of creation.*

Gentle, comforting Spirit,
cooling and refreshing
as the welcoming summer breeze,
**You call us together**
**offering us your calm reassurance.**

Teasing, mischievous Spirit,
whipping up litter
in playful eddies in the street,
**You call us together**
**inviting us to join your whirlwind dance.**

Strong, demanding Spirit,
certain and assured
as the persuasive, blustery gale,
**You call us together**
**challenging us to reconciliation and change.**

Awesome, powerful Spirit,
destructive and creative
as the terrifying beauty of the raging storm,
**You call us together**
**inspiring us to embody your vision of Shalom.**

# Hiding Behind Mummy's Skirt

*Sometimes even the noisiest, most confident child when faced with a new situation will hide behind mummy's skirt. They then have to be gently coaxed out or, on occasion, some stronger persuasion is needed until they become their usual noisy, endearing personality again. It's not only children who can lack confidence. Sometimes we need some gentle persuasion too.*

Your spirit billows around us
bringing warmth
as we huddle inside ourselves
bracing ourselves against the world.

Your spirit eddies around us
nudgingly teasing
as we are enticed to peek out
seeing the world with new eyes.

Your spirit whirlwinds around us
rushing and forceful
as we are blown out of our insularity
meeting the eyes of the people around us.

Forgive us
when we hide ourselves away
content with our own lives
oblivious to the lives of others.

Breathe in us
and breathe your life through us
catch us up in your whirlwind dance of life
that in community we may be life.

# Dare We...

Our paths merge, touching, meeting,
encountering the other,
different textures and tapestries of life,
vibrant songs and rhythmic dances,
stilled ... to humble silence.

Our eyes take in the richness of beauty,
our created world ,
shining sun,
rippling water,
the gentle, whispering breeze,
the coolness of wet earth,
rushing fire,
hard stones,
destructive forces ...
or life-affirming possibility.

A beggar's bowl
pleads, implores,
entices, demands,
invites us to look ...
to see the violence and poverty
of that which is beautiful ...
the fragility of life itself.

Our eyes meet,
alive and glistening,
vision clearing
as we contemplate
the candle
that is not lit.

Dare we ...
dare we risk playing
in the crackle of fire?
dare we risk touching
the hard edges of our lives?
dare we risk seeing ourselves,
in the mirror of the bowl?
dare we risk toppling
the pillars of our fearful arrogance?
dare we kindle the flame of hope?

Shanti,
Salaam,
Shalom,
Pacem,

... for a moment
peace is with us.

143

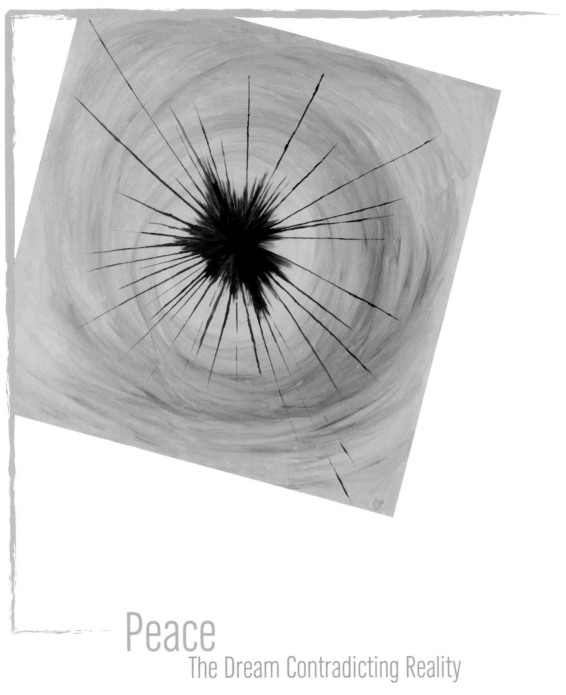

Peace
The Dream Contradicting Reality

*B of the Bang* is Thomas Heatherwick's magnificent sculpture outside the City of Manchester Stadium in East Manchester. Inspired by the words of athlete Linford Christie, who spoke of the need to start on 'the b of the bang', it is a great explosion of energy, hope and new life in the midst of our community.

Deborah painted this abstract picture in January 2005 and when Imogen saw it, she immediately christened it 'BoftheBang'.

My abiding memory of the Commonwealth Games, for which the stadium was designed, is of a rain-soaked people of Manchester carrying twinkling paper lanterns into the darkened stadium. The lanterns were shaped as the domes, minarets and spires of ethereal buildings to represent the different faiths and communities of Manchester. These came together and 'danced' in the belly of the stadium before carrying their light outwards into the Manchester night.

As the eucharist ends, we go out to share the peace we have received with the wider world. Peace, the impossible dream. Peace, the folly of protesters demonstrating against a war. Peace, the hope that will not die. Peace, the dream that cannot be killed. Resurrection.

# Flowers in the Desert

*Our regeneration process has been delayed yet again by political manœuvring at the Town Hall. Advent, the time of looking forward from the darkness towards the flickering flame of hope, has a particular resonance. We believe there is hope. Hope against hope. To hope is to be the prophet crying in the wilderness. Things can be different. Things will be different. Things must be different.*

We wait, we long for, we hope,
reality seems dark as night,
drab as the peeling paint,
dowdy as damp-ridden houses.

We wait, we long for, we hope,
peace seems a long-forgotten dream,
as wars continue to rage,
as people die from hunger and bullets.

We wait, we long for, we hope,
as Herod seeks out a new-born child,
soldiers searching from house to house,
the wail of mourning rife in Judea.

We wait, we long for, we hope,
as the new-born child grows to maturity,
itinerant healer and teller of stories,
touching the outcast and the lost.

We wait, we long for, we hope,
as hope itself seems to die,
the saviour hangs on a cross,
a tomb's silence deafening the skies.

And as we wait, as we long for, as we hope,
we look for the signs,
daring to believe there is hope,
dreaming of a miracle.

And as we wait, as we long for, as we hope,
the signs of heaven on earth are here
in the breaking of bread
and the pouring of wine.

In the rising of a bright star in the East
we see glimpses of God's Shalom,
and the desert is imbued
with the delicate fragrance
of flowers pushing up through the earth.

In the journeying of exotic travellers
we see glimpses of God's Shalom,
and the desert is permeated
with the inspiring melody
of birdsong wafting in the air.

In the birth of a baby in a stable
we see glimpses of God's Shalom,
and the desert is infused
with the riotous extravagance
of flowers bursting into bloom.

In the arrival of rugged shepherds
we see glimpses of God's Shalom,
and the desert is saturated
with the gentle drenching of spring rains
as they hit the scorched earth.

147

In the eyes of refugees at play
we see glimpses of God's Shalom,
and the desert is refreshed
by the earthy aroma
of warm, wet soil.

We wait, we long for, we hope
and in the waiting, in the longing, in the
    hoping,
we take plain, simple bread,
sign of Christ's body
broken for the life of the world.

We wait, we long for, we hope
and in the waiting, in the longing, in the
    hoping,
we take rich, full-bodied wine,
sign of wonder and celebration
the promise of Shalom for the world.

So we continue to wait, to long for, to hope,
to look for glimpses of God's Shalom,
when the desert shall be infused
with the riotous extravagance
of flowers bursting into bloom.

# B of the Bang

*On Boxing Day we had decided to look at the theme of surprises as in opening presents, an almost white Christmas, and the recently constructed* B of the Bang *sculpture. News was just breaking of an earthquake under the sea and tidal waves engulfing villages in Asia, reminding us that surprises are not always pleasant. Rather bleary-eyed, this was my attempt to try and make sense of it all. Although we now know the scale of the Tsunami disaster, this prayer remains in this hopeful chapter as a reminder that even the greatest tragedy cannot destroy our hope.*

God-of-surprises,
You delight us
by creating a magical winter world
where the pinky orange glow of sunrise
kisses the freshly fallen snow;
where icicles hang suspended by drainpipes
and footprints crunch in circles around
    back yards.

God-of-surprises,
You amaze us
in the sheer scale of *B of the Bang*
in the overwhelming beauty of purple
    and green hues
transforming harsh, rust-coloured steel
into delicate shards of starlight
exploding across the heavens.

God-of-surprises,
You astound us
in the yearning for justice of a teenager's song
fulfilled in the bustle and din of a baby's birth;
where the sacredness of the moment
is brought down to earth and cradled
in the rough-cut straw of an animal's
    feeding trough.

God-of-surprises,
You dumbfound us
in premiering the good news chorale
to lowly shepherds on a rural hillside;
enticing exotic travellers with signs in the stars
to celebrate and ponder together
the miracle of new life, God with us.

God-of-surprises,
You jolt us out of our complacency
with the evil scheming of a jealous king,
the shifting of tectonic plates deep
    in the earth
and walls of water engulfing villages;
in the hurried packing of refugees
and arrival of new faces in our communities.

God-of-surprises,
You shock us
by holding a mirror up to the evil of our world;
the baby maturing to controversial adulthood
shaking us awake with stories and signs
    of God's love;
bread broken and wine poured,
'This is my body, this is my blood.'

And so, God-of-surprises,
we celebrate your presence with us
in broken bread and poured-out wine
remembering our brokenness
celebrating your presence in community
yet longing for the wholeness of your Shalom.

God-of-surprises,
astonish us
with the sheer beauty of your world
shake us
to challenge all that mars that beauty
and blow us away
with the hope of beauty restored in
    community.

# Old Spider

*In the closing reflections of my thesis I began to dream using images, metaphors and poetry of a world beyond oppression and environmental devastation where the voices and wisdom that had accompanied my journey would be heard and valued.*

The Old Spider
Weaves Dreams
into the
Web of Life
its myriad of threads
glistening
in the Moonshine

The mysterious Moon
Spins Wisdom
from the
Stories of Experience
its ebbing and flowing
quickened
by an Eagle's shadow

The soaring Eagle
Inspires Vision
ReConnecting
Earth and Sky
its changing perception
challenged
by Earth's destruction

Old Spider,
mysterious Moon,
soaring Eagle
teach us
to Re-discover
our Selves
we are Earth.

# daring to speak

*Rubem Alves, the Brazilian theologian/philosopher/ psychoanalyst, writes of words which are good to eat. As we taste bread and wine, we also savour the words with which we express our faith. Human language can never be adequate to express God, yet communication is fundamental to who we are. We dare to speak, but all our speaking is open and provisional. Authentic speech can never be used to close off, exclude or suppress. Words which are good enough to eat are changing and transitory. They express a moment, a thought, a feeling. As soon as they are uttered, they are changed by being heard.*

unspoken word
god of music and dance
who cannot be defined
gather us in your presence
gather us as your presence
for we proclaim what we cannot understand
that the creator of all that is
all that has been
all that will be
is present
alive
among us now
foolishly
dancing
in our thoughts
and our prayers
forgive us we pray
when we try to define you
when we try to pin down your random spirit
who blows where she wishes
when we dare to speak
in your unnameable name
of that which we cannot understand
in our misunderstanding
make yourself known
and love us into becoming

# Simple Eucharist

*A recipe book might have recipes for a 'basic tomato sauce', or 'béchamel', the classic dishes which become the cook's vocabulary. This eight-voice eucharist was a very early attempt to define the building blocks of our liturgy in relation to modern life.*

1. Let us gather together
2. from north and south
3. from east and west
4. from countries far
5. from communities near
6. from our houses and flats
7. from our wider families
8. from our neighbours and friends

**To share this meal together**

2. Let us give thanks for bread
5. wheat harvested
8. grain threshed
7. flour and yeast mixed
3. dough kneaded
1. bread baked
6. loaves packaged
4. groceries bought

**This is my body broken for you**

7. Let us give thanks for wine
6. vines tended
2. fruit picked
8. grapes crushed
3. juice fermented
1. liquid bottled
5. crates transported
4. vintage selected

**This is my blood shed for you**

5. Let us remember
1. earth polluted
8. farmers struggling
2. labourers exploited
4. hauliers protesting
7. factories closing
3. supermarkets gaining
6. divisions growing

**I will make a new relationship with you**

4. Let us tell the story
8. friends gathered
6. a meal shared
1. memories made
7. leaders plotting
2. soldiers arresting
3. a man dying
5. God crying

**Do this in memory of me**

6. Let us celebrate
2. the texture of bread
8. sign of new life
4. the taste of wine
1. sign of a new relationship
5. let us celebrate
7. the gift of friendship
3. and God's love for us

**Let us eat and be thankful**

151

# Hot Cross Eucharist

*Hot, cross eucharist might describe our feelings as we struggle to pray amid the chaos. In this case, however, it refers to the hot cross buns which Beth (then aged two) and Tim had made the day before. Unfortunately, the buns were indeed 'a pile of shiny pebbles', beautiful to look at but as hard as rocks to eat.*

A pile of shiny pebbles,
Precious jewels of love.
The stone the builders rejected
Has become the chief cornerstone.

Flour –
Dull and uninteresting
Yeast –
The leaven of life
Currants –
Grapes with the life squeezed out of them
Sugar –
Sweetens the bitter pill
Spices –
Far away and mysterious

And into each precious jewel
Is slashed the cross
Of bitter pain and betrayal.

With friends and companions,
When the triumph was over,
Jesus sat down to feast.
A feast of fools
A feast of fun
A feast of celebration.

And when the feast was ended
Jesus took a piece of bread
Not ordinary bread

Unleavened bread
Special bread
Celebration bread
He gave thanks
Rejoicing
And broke the bread
Tearfully
Saying:
This is my body broken for you.

Afterwards, he took a cup of the wine,
Crushed from so many grapes,
That we might rejoice,
And shared it with his betrayer.
This cup seals my love for you.

As we share this special bread,
Holy bread,
Broken for us all,
May our lives embody your love.

As we drink this wine,
Poured out for all to share,
May our lives celebrate your beauty.

This is the death we remember.
This is the new life we celebrate.
This is the vision we proclaim.

So, foolish God,
advocate of justice in a world of injustice,
peacemaker in a world of violence,
lover in a world of hate,
unite us in celebration of your foolishness;
take these gifts of bread and wine
and transform them
into the signs and seals of your Shalom
and a foretaste of the heavenly banquet
in which we shall all share.

# What If...

What if... the women keeping vigil at the foot
of the cross
witnessed not the cruel, senseless
death of a revolutionary
but the torture and crucifixion of
many people's lives?

What if... the women crying outside a garden
tomb
mourned not the emptiness and
loss of a teacher
but the silencing and annihilation of
many people's lives?

What if... the women shocked into talking
with angels
spoke not of the disappearance of
the body of a healer
but proclaimed the presence of the
risen Christ?

**He is here, his presence is with us.**

What if... heaven and hell are not dreams
beyond the grave
but realities here and now?

What if... death is not revenge at the hands
of an angry god
but the embracing of suffering by
Christ's outstretched arms?

What if... crucifixion is not the passive
acceptance of a father's will
but our struggle to overcome
violence and injustice?

**He is here, his presence is with us.**

What if... women flinging insults and abuse
across the Holy Cross divide
can form a friendship based on
trust and the beginnings of
understanding?

What if... instead of smiling with veiled eyes
across a clinic waiting room
we could share the joys and
frustrations of shaping a new life?

What if... instead of merely nodding to my
Asian neighbour
our children could become friends?

**He is here, his presence is with us.**

What if... the work of caring and nurturing
was valued
more than juggling figures on a
page?

What if... the peace keepers put down
their guns
and became peace and justice
makers?

What if... we didn't just share bread around a
piece of church furniture
but had the courage to share bread
across the world?

No 'what ifs...?' We have rolled back the stone.
He is here, his presence is in us and among us
The peace of the risen Christ be with you.
**And also with you.**

# A Glimpse of God?

I looked up into the sky
and all I saw were clouds and the sun
I didn't see God.
At night I looked up
and all I saw were stars and the moon
I didn't see God.

I looked into a great cathedral
with stained-glass windows and statues of saints
but I didn't see God.
I looked at the mighty bell tower
at the beautiful gargoyles and flying buttresses
but I didn't see God.

I looked to the hills
so grand and so green
but I didn't see God.
I looked into the forest
proud, dark and mysterious
but I didn't see God.

So I came home
and saw a child,
sharing bread with an old woman,
and there I saw God.
I saw you, rather scared,
reach out and touch
an unlovely stranger
and in your eyes
and in your soul
I saw the living
dancing
celebrating
God.
May I join you this morning
in worship?

# Welcoming the Stranger

*Like many inner city areas, Openshaw is changing. Where, until recently, the majority in our community was white British working class, we now meet people who have been settled here from many parts of the world. While this brings a few tensions, this 'rainbow community' brings stability, skills and vibrancy.*

God of justice and of love,
We praise you for the richness and diversity of our own community,
Where people from many races now bustle around our streets,
Where different languages can be heard in our local shops,
We praise you for the wealth of skills and knowledge
Those who seek refuge bring to our community,
Where we can sample food from many different countries,
Where our children learn about different customs and religious festivals.

God of justice and of love,
We confess that as a community
We are not always welcoming of asylum seekers and refugees,
We are not always understanding of the situations that bring people to our country.
We confess that we too as part of this community
Have not done as much as we could
To make people feel wanted and loved,
And acknowledge our own assumptions and prejudices.

God of justice and of love,
Forgive us and challenge us
To stand up against our government and media
When they stereotype refugees and asylum seekers,
To speak up against the racism and ignorance of our own community,
Forgive us and challenge us
To become more welcoming to our neighbours from different races,
To be more open to their situations and life stories.

# Dream-catcher God

*Clare wrote this prayer to celebrate Beth's third birthday and 'presentation' ceremony. Using a large hoop, ribbons and beads, family and friends wove something of their hopes and dreams for Beth into a dream-catcher which now hangs above her bed. While the prayer reflects Beth's unique personality, it could easily be adapted to celebrate another unique personality.*

Dream-catcher God,
you spin the memories of our lives...
the first glimpse into new-born eyes,
the first sleepy, milk-filled smile,
the first faltering tiny steps,
the sleepless nights,
the irritability and tears of teething,
the heal-kicking of the temper tantrum.
Help us to hold on to our memories of (name)
as we watch her develop her own,
   distinct personality.

Dream-catcher God,
you spin the stories of our lives...
the exuberance of running and tumbling,
the excitement of celebrating birthdays,
the exploration of new ideas,
the determination of achieving
   the next milestone,
the incessant desire to communicate,
the endless questions through which we learn.
We thank you for the person (name)
   has become
and for what she contributes to each
   of our lives.

Dream-catcher God,
you spin the dreams that give meaning
   to our lives...
the laughter and tears that forge friendships,
the learning from previous generations that
   teach us of our past,
the discovering of the quirkiness of the
   natural world,
the appreciating of a rich diversity of cultures,
the desire to contribute to the regeneration
   of community,
the hope for a world that lives in justice
   and peace.
We share our hopes and our dreams
   with (name)
knowing we set her free to travel on
   her own journey.

Dream-catcher God,
Teach us to treasure the memories we have,
Help us to share our stories with one another,
And inspire us to spin our dreams
   into our future.

# Pink Lemonade

*One of the problems of worship in the inner city is that much of our worship material assumes a rural 'idyll'. It might seem strange, therefore, to include this picture prayer in a chapter growing out of our inner city reality. But there is beauty here. The 'umbrellared tables' might be the cheap plastic picnic tables with beer adverts on the parasols, but they are a joyous celebration of summer in the city. Summer in the city is a time when people sit on their doorsteps, park babies outside in their buggies and local teenagers are surprised to find that you can eat the blackberries that grow on the railway embankment.*

God of the summer sun
and cool breezes we thank and praise you
for the warmth of summer
for rustling leaves and creaking branches
for the chink of glasses and smokiness of BBQs
for babies in baggy nappies and floppy sun hats
for football and picnics in the park
we thank and praise you
for fish-shaped ice cubes bobbing in pink lemonade
and for bicycle rides along the canal
for juicy berries picked by the railway embankment
and for t-shirts dancing on the washing line
for umbrellared tables outside cafés
we thank and praise you
for freedom to go out without fear of the dark
for chattering birds swooping in to roost
for children squealing
in the
playground
and adults
passing the
time of day
on park
benches
God of the
summer
sun and
cool breezes
we thank and praise you

# Winter Eucharist

*Winter in the city is a long, miserable drag. Bright, crisp snow scenes and great winter skies are for Christmas cards and the imagination. In Manchester, people huddle under bus shelters to hide from the seemingly endless rain.*

*Candles have come to symbolize the foolish gospel hope which refuses to die in the face of the despair all around. A flicker of hope in the gloom.*

*Be careful, though. Not once, but twice, we have left candles burning and come back just in time to prevent complete disaster. Fortunately, a brown ring on the carpet and a shattered window were the only casualties!*

Into the vandalism
and deprivation
of our city streets –
a candle is lit

Into the fear
and violence
of conflict –
a candle is lit

Into the icy grip
of a long
hard winter –
a candle is lit

Into the drabness
and into the depths
of depression –
a candle is lit

a candle is lit –
a welcome
and hospitality
for the wanderer.

a candle is lit –
the intensity of heat
forging swords
into ploughshares.

a candle is lit –
the first stirrings
in the waking earth
preparing for new life.

a candle is lit –
the burst of energy
creating our visions
turning dreams into reality.

On the night
they betrayed him
Jesus welcomed
his friends
offering hospitality
at his table
food for the journey
bread and wine.

On the night
swords were drawn
Jesus embodied
non-violence,
This is my body
given for you
This is my blood
shed for you.

On the night
hope was buried
Jesus spoke
words of life,
bread of heaven
uniting us all,
wine of the earth
celebrating relatedness.

On the night
God was silent
Jesus walked the path
of risk and vulnerability,
waiting for the stirrings
of Divine Wisdom
the creative spark
of Divine Inspiration.

So Jesus invites us
and welcomes us,
to be transformed
and to transform our world,
to be alive
to the new life within us,
and to dream our world
into a place of justice and peace.

We are people of winter,
a people of faith,
who wait through the long cold nights,
who hold on when hoping seems in vain,
but above all we are people who hope,
who dream of a better world,
who celebrate glimpses of God's Shalom,
embraced by one whose love will not let us go.

# Fast Track Urban World

*Funding deadlines, meetings, collecting children from school, football practice, gymnastics, more meetings and even the occasional meeting crowd in on us. We were obviously particularly tired this week! But in the end there is/will be Shalom.*

in our fast track urban world
everything happens here and now
advertising hoardings offer us the latest products
with more and more functions
that will perform ever faster and more efficiently
we live in an 'I want' society
where everything should have been done yesterday
where it is easier to take out a loan for five thousand pounds
than it is to open a children's savings account
where the papers debate a looming pensions crisis
because we are too busy living for today
to think about providing for our future

into this fast track urban world
in danger of losing its soul to the hedonism of the moment
where we have no time to build community
and barely know our next door neighbours
God speaks a different wisdom
a language of being rather than doing
of patience rather than hurry
of people rather than products
a wisdom of peace and non-violence
a language of walking the long journey of justice
across the bounds of time and place
a grounded identity challenging our lifestyles of constant change

into this fast track urban world
Jesus embarks on his journey towards Jerusalem
travelling the highways of Israel Palestine
his face set with determination to complete the journey
embarked on over three years before
accompanied by those society sought to exclude
into this urban world marked by imperial status and power
of grand architecture and unregulated markets

Jesus is carried on a donkey
an impromptu people's celebration
where the wholeness of people's lives and relationships
are singled out and celebrated as signs of Shalom

into this fast track urban world
Jesus takes a simple loaf of unleavened bread
takes time to give thanks to the One who created it
breaks it and shares it among them
this is my body broken by your fast track urban world
where a person's life is expendable in the race for money and power
into this fast track urban world
Jesus takes a cup of celebratory wine
takes time to lift it and savours it
and shares it among them
this is my blood spilt by the violence of broken relationships
given that you might learn to live together in restored community

In this fast track urban world
We pause to give thanks,
to stop and reflect on the stories of God's people,
on the stories that both shape our world
and challenge us to think again.
We pause to take, eat and savour the bread
and confess our caught-up-ness
in the whirlwind of our world.
We pause to take, drink and savour the wine
and look again at the faces of the people around us,
the community of which we are a part
and to commit again to walk together in your Shalom.

# This Moment

*Many years ago, Mersey Street belonged to a local group of churches. For complicated, political reasons, the church had to leave the group. As part of our storytelling, narrative work, we decided to rekindle that relationship. One Sunday we held a joint service. We all made and shared bread together.*

Let us not take bread for granted
Let us take time to give thanks
Thanks for this moment
Nature bursting into bloom
Wheat seeds germinating
Shoots pushing through the soil
Yeast fermenting
A celebration of life.

Let us not take bread for granted
Let us take time to give thanks
Thanks for this moment
People chatting on doorsteps
Friends playing bowls in the park
Children skipping in playgrounds
Strangers smiling
A celebration of life.

Let us not take bread for granted
Let us take time to give thanks
Thanks for this moment
Crowds walking for life
Placards raised in protest
Fair trade coffee sold in supermarkets
Questions raised
A celebration of life.

Let us not take bread for granted
Let us take time to give thanks
Thanks for this moment
This time and place
For friendships rekindled
Memories shared
New relationships begun
A celebration of life.

# Hide and Seek

*Psalm 139 is an important psalm for us. At Rachel's presentation, her godfather, Martin Scott, sang the hymn he had written based upon this psalm. It was a joyful expression of our wonder at her birth. The next time Martin performed this song for us was at Tim Clay's funeral. Our hopes and dreams had been snatched from us and the psalm had become an angry lament. Years later, we re-visited the psalm. This eucharist was the result.*

God, you have searched us and know us.
You know when we sit down and when we rise.
You know when we sit down at table
**for you are already here.**
This is your table
**for you are already here.**
Before us and behind us
**you are already here.**
In heights, in depths
**you are already here.**
In darkness and light
**you are already here.**

This is your table;
we are your guests.
**We are your guests.**
We sit at the table
**We sit at your table.**

At your table
not under it,
cowering as from attack.
At your table
children, sharing supper
playing hide and seek.
At table
Under table
You, the seeker, find us.
**You, the seeker of the lost**
You, the seeker of the lonely
**You, the seeker of the small**
You, the seeker of the insignificant
You find us
**You find us lying in a manger**
**And change the world for ever**
**through us.**

On the night hope died
a man sat down at table with those he
 thought were his friends.
He tried to wash their feet which made
 them feel silly.
One of them tried to hide away,
 but he sought him out and said,
unless you let me wash your feet,
 you have no part of me.

Then he dipped bread with the one who
 would cut him to the quick
and destroy his trust in human nature.

Finally, he took a piece of bread and
 when his betrayer had left,
he shared it with his friends, saying
This is my body, broken for you.
Eat it to share in my dying.
Later, he took a cup of wine, gave it to
 them and said,
This is the new relationship with God.
Sin and death cannot break it,
for it is sealed by my blood.
Drink and be part of me,
For ever.

So we do not hide.
For you know us
and in our brokenness
are united with us.
**One**
in love
**One**
in acceptance
**One**
in trust.
Send us out
in the unbreakable hope
of your love
to re-make ourselves
and re-create the world
in your image
**this day**
**and for ever.**

163

# Triumphal Entry?

*Triumph is not a word we use very much. Fifteen years ago, when church membership had declined to around four, a meeting was called to close the church. It made no sense humanly speaking to stay open but to close would have been a sign that God had deserted the inner city and the people here. This eucharist based on Zechariah 9.9-12 and the title of the song 'The Greatness of the Small', celebrates the foolish love of God which does indeed treasure the small.*

*We can hear the headlines*
*hooting with laughter and disappointment:*
'Jesus makes an ass of himself!'
'Jesus the jester rides again!'
'What is God playing at?'
'Would-be Messiah misses the mark!'

**And we dream of a miracle, because we know the greatness of the small.**

*But behind the clamour of jeering, mocking voices we can hear the still small voices gaining in courage:*
'Jesus walks a path of non-violence'
'Political power turned on its head'
'Can Wisdom grow out of divine foolishness?'
'Swords beaten into ploughshares.'

**And we dream of a miracle, because we know the greatness of the small.**

*And we hear the world stopped in its tracks desiring yet fearing the path to peace:*
'Servants take the place of honour at feast'
'Poor inherit the earth in will left by our creator'
'Has heaven been glimpsed on earth?'
'Exclusive religious club opens its doors'

**And we dream of a miracle, because we know the greatness of the small.**

*Earthly God,*
*on the night when everything seemed*
*to go wrong,*
*on the night when the air was filled*
*with anything but peace,*
*on the night swords were drawn*
*and tempers flared,*
*on the night before the ultimate act*
*of violence,*
*you celebrated with your friends the freedom*
*of the Passover story,*
*confronting them with the reality of*
*imprisonment and death,*
*yet entrusting them to continue your work of*
*healing and justice-making*
*and promising them your peace.*

**And we dream of a miracle, because we know the greatness of the small.**

*Vulnerable God,*
*On that night you took the simplest of bread,*
*gave thanks for that which we take*
*for granted,*
*and tore it apart, as violence tears*
*our world apart,*
*saying, this is my body given for you.*

**And we dream of a miracle, because we know the greatness of the small.**

Suffering God,
On that night you took the richest of wine,
gave thanks for that which now causes us so
   much debate,
and poured it into a common cup, as blood is
   commonly shed in human conflict,
saying, this wine is the new relationship
   with God.

**And we dream of a miracle, because we
know the greatness of the small.**

*We offer you praise our foolish God,*
*who shows our wisdom to be empty words,*
*and our systems to be built on war and injustice,*
*who feeds us with the grains from the*
   *one bread,*
*and nourishes us with wine from the one vine.*

**And we dream of a miracle, because we
know the greatness of the small.**

We offer you praise our daring God,
who shows us a different way,
startles us with creative solutions,
challenges us to resolve conflict,
and to dream the impossible into reality.

**And we dream of a miracle, because we
know the greatness of the small.**

Therefore with the whole earth around us
we celebrate your glory, for ever praising
   you and saying:
Holy, holy, holy,
vulnerable God,
earth as heaven is full of your glory,
hosanna to the one who rides a donkey,
blessed is the one who comes in the
   name of love,
hosanna to the one who brings us peace.

**And we dream of a miracle, because we
know the greatness of the small.**

**And we dare to dream of a miracle,
because we know the greatness of the
small and the wisdom of the holy.**

# Living the Dream

*The blessing at the end of the service is what connects the dream which we have tasted in bread and wine with the reality of daily life.*

May the blessing of the God
of peace and justice
be with us;
May the blessing of the Son
who weeps the tears of the world's suffering
be with us;
May the blessing of the Spirit
who inspires us to reconciliation and hope
be with us;
from now into eternity.

May the blessing of the God who danced
at the dawning of creation
**dance with us.**

May the blessing of the Son who challenges us to dance
the pain of the world's suffering
**dance with us.**

And may the blessing of the Spirit who invites us to dance
with her in the dance of celebration
**dance with us
from now into eternity.**

May the blessing of the God
who flung the sun and moon across the heavens
bring you joy and warmth.
May the blessing of the child
whose birth was heralded by a star
guide your feet in paths of justice and peace.
And may the blessing of the Spirit
who dreamed at the dawning of an Easter morning
fill your dreams with longing and hope,
until dreams become reality.

May the blessing of the God who gives us bread,
the blessing of the Son who breaks the bread,
and the blessing of the Holy Spirit
who challenges us to share bread with the world,
Be with us all.

May the gentle Spirit comfort and hold us,
May the playful Spirit laugh and dance with us,
May the challenging Spirit re-create and transform us,
May the inspiring Spirit hold us in her dreams.

# Notes

Prayers were first published as follows:
Geoffrey Duncan (ed.), *A Lifetime of Blessing*, Canterbury Press, 2004
Waiting in the Womb (co-written with David Sutcliffe); Joy of New Life; Grounded God

Geoffrey Duncan (ed.), *Timeless Prayers for Peace*, Canterbury Press, 2004
Enough Room for Everyone; Longing for Peace; Remembrance Confession

Geoffrey Duncan (ed.), *Courage to Love*, Darton, Longman and Todd, 2002
Embodying the Word (co-written with Lis Mullen)

*Roots Worship*, Roots for Churches Limited, Issue 10, Mar./ Apr. 2004
Journeying Towards the Cross; Journey to the Cross; Humble God; Beauty Poured Out; May the
    blessing of the God of peace and justice; May the blessing of the God who danced

*Roots Worship*, Roots for Churches Limited, Issue 19, Sep./ Oct. 2005
What Is on the Inside; Shrek; How Can We?; Autumn Thanksgiving; Consciousness; ASBO Prayer; Look
    Around You; Hope Against Hope; no borders; Beaufort Spirit; Welcoming the Stranger

Janet Lees (ed.), *Justice, Joy & Jubilee*, The United Reformed Church, 1999
The Call of Wisdom; The Path to Emmaus; May the blessing of the God who gives us bread

Natalie Watson, Hanna Strack and Brigitte Enzner-Probst, *The Women's Christian Yearbook* 2002,
    Canterbury Press, 2001
Pink Lemonade

Christian Aid (comp.), *Pocket Prayers for Peace and Justice*, Church House Publishing, 2004
Journey to the Cross; May the blessing of the God of peace and justice

http://www.rootsontheweb.com
Enough Room for Everyone; Longing for Peace; Let us go from here (co-written with Jill Thornton);
    May the blessing of the extravagant God; Re-storation; Heartbeat of the Earth

The following prayers were first written for *Encircling Prayer*, the Luther King House Prayer Book:
Look Around You; Embodying the Word (co-written with Lis Mullen); Pink Lemonade

Miriam's Sister was co-written with Jess Uden
Eucharist for an Autumn Equinox draws upon imagery from the reflection 'Women of Autumn',
    Miriam Therese Winter, *WomanWitness*, Crossroad, 1992

The Swirling Whirling Waters; Enemy of Apathy Blessing and Enemy of Apathy all draw upon imagery from the song 'Enemy of Apathy' from the Iona Community, *Enemy of Apathy*, Wild Goose Publications, 1988

Dancing Fool quotes Frank Zappa, 'Dancing Fool' from the album *Sheik Yerbouti*, Rykodisc, 1979 (permission sought)

Triumphal Entry? draws on the song 'The Greatness of the Small' from *Love from Below*, Wild Goose Publications, 1989

# Index of First Lines and Titles